D1770707

LETTERS OF NOTE: CATS

Letters of Note was born in 2009 with the launch of lettersofnote.com, a website celebrating old-fashioned correspondence that has since been visited over 100 million times. The first *Letters of Note* volume was published in October 2013, followed later that year by the first Letters Live, an event at which world-class performers delivered remarkable letters to a live audience.

Since then, these two siblings have grown side by side, with *Letters of Note* becoming an international phenomenon, and Letters Live shows being staged at iconic venues around the world, from London's Royal Albert Hall to the theatre at the Ace Hotel in Los Angeles.

You can find out more at lettersofnote.com and letterslive.com. And now you can also listen to the audio editions of the new series of *Letters of Note*, read by an extraordinary cast drawn from the wealth of talent that regularly takes part in the acclaimed Letters Live shows.

Letters of Note

CATS

COMPILED BY

Shaun Usher

PENGUIN BOOKS

For Kala, Dodi, Gavin, Stacey, Silvie,
Polo and Chico

PENGUIN BOOKS
An imprint of Penguin Random House LLC
penguinrandomhouse.com

First published in Great Britain by Canongate Books Ltd 2020
Published in Penguin Books 2020

Compliation and introduction copyright © 2020 by Shaun Usher
Penguin supports copyright. Copyright fuels creativity, encourages diverse voices, promotes free speech, and creates a vibrant culture. Thank you for buying an authorized edition of this book and for complying with copyright laws by not reproducing, scanning, or distributing any part of it in any form without permission. You are supporting writers and allowing Penguin to continue to publish books for every reader.

Pages 129–130 constitute an extension of this copyright page.

Library of Congress Control Number: 2020940584
ISBN 9780143134664 (paperback)
ISBN 9780525506478 (ebook)

Printed in the United States of America
1 3 5 7 9 10 8 6 4 2

Set in Joanna MT Std

CONTENTS

A letter is a time bomb, a message in a bottle, a spell, a cry for help, a story, an expression of concern, a ladle of love, a way to connect through words. This simple and brilliantly democratic art form remains a potent means of communication and, regardless of whatever technological revolution we are in the middle of, the letter lives and, like literature, it always will.

INTRODUCTION

For many thousands of years, since human beings first began domesticating cats and dogs – for reasons of pest control and hunting respectively – there has been one particular question consistently on the lips of the population that has never failed to divide its audience straight down the middle:

CATS OR DOGS?

As the proud owner of multiple iterations of both since childhood, some more appealing than others, admittedly, it is plainly obvious to me that the correct answer, and in fact the only logical answer, is yes, because to choose between cats and dogs is to choose between food and drink: pointless, and likely to change depending on the time of day and current mood. For now, though, let us focus on our feline friends of this world, hundreds of millions of which are currently members of human families across the globe, slinking around the ankles of their two-legged housemates, purring loudly as they wait for breakfast, kneading soft furnishings with a look of such ecstasy that one cannot help but wish to swap roles if only for a minute, gracefully leaping through the air across impossible distances to escape the clumsy child with no boundaries to speak of, casually bopping the nose of the overexcited and intellectually inferior dog who shares the kitchen, somehow opening that cupboard door that leads to the treats, elegantly sauntering through the home with an air of arrogance that makes one wonder who has domesticated whom and, actually, hang on a moment, have we all been stitched up?

In this volume, you will discover that we owe one particular cat a huge debt of gratitude for inspiring one of history's most influential scientists to improve our lives immeasurably. You will learn about a musical instrument that was to be powered by cats. You will learn of a legally dubious business plan involving a steady supply of cats, rats and snakes, all for a very healthy profit. You will learn about supernatural double-tailed Japanese cats. You will learn about the cat who brought a much-needed smile to the face of a young girl hiding from the worst of humankind. You will learn about the Illinois governor who with great panache saved the cat community from intense embarrassment. You will learn about a poem written by one of the greats in memory of a cat who fell into a fishbowl. You will learn about the cat who defecated into a tissue box belonging to a famous novelist – a novelist who, at the time, as luck would have it, had a cold.

You will learn all these things, and more, through the time capsule we call the letter – humans' most precious, enjoyable and endangered form of communication, currently being nudged towards the sorting office in the sky by the many digital, charmless, fugacious alternatives that invade our every waking thought, reducing our relationships to something far less meaningful. Indeed, my hopes for this book are two-fold: to further intensify your love for these magnificent animals, if that is even possible, and to remind you that without letters these stories would likely have died a quick death, never to be retold, and that we owe it to ourselves, and future generations, and all these cats who deserve and, let's face it, demand recognition, to write more letters.

So please do exactly that. Take ten minutes out of your day. Find a piece of paper, rescue your last remaining pen from the cat, and write to someone, if only to let them know that you are thinking of them. There's a chance, albeit slim, that you may even get a reply.

Shaun Usher

2020

P.S. Please send me a copy.

The Letters

LETTER 01
IS NATURE A GIGANTIC CAT?

Nikola Tesla to Pola Fotić

23 July 1939

Born in 1856 in Smiljan, in Croatia, Nikola Tesla was an inventor whose invaluable impact on the modern world is difficult to comprehend. During the course of his eighty-six years he made numerous breakthroughs in the realm of electrical engineering, particularly around his AC induction motor, and by the time of his death, the 'Father of Electricity' had approximately 300 patents to his name. In Washington DC in 1939, aged eighty-three and in failing health, Tesla met Pola Fotić, the daughter of the Yugoslav ambassador to the United States, and they bonded over their shared love of cats. Soon afterwards, from his home in New York City, Tesla wrote to his new friend and revealed the reason behind his lifelong fascination with electricity.

THE LETTER

New York,
July 23, 1939

My Dear Miss Fotić,
I am forwarding to you the "Calendar of Yugoslavia" of 1939 showing the house and community in which I had many sad and joyful adventures, and in which also, by a bizarre coincidence, I was born. As you see from the photograph on the sheet for June, the old-fashioned building is located at the foot of a wooded hill called Bogdanic. Adjoining it is a church and behind it, a little further up, a graveyard. Our nearest neighbors were two miles away. In the winter, when the snow was six or seven feet deep, our isolation was complete.

My mother was indefatigable. She worked regularly from four o'clock in the morning till eleven in the evening. From four to breakfast time – six a.m. – while others slumbered, I never closed my eyes but watched my mother with intense pleasure as she attended quickly – sometimes running – to her many self-imposed duties. She directed the servants to take care of all our domestic animals, she milked the cows, she performed all sorts of labor unassisted, set the table, prepared breakfast for the whole household. Only when it was ready to be served did the rest of the family get up. After breakfast everybody followed my mother's inspiring example. All did their work diligently, liked it, and so achieved a measure of contentment.

But I was the happiest of all, the fountain of my enjoyment being our magnificent Máčak – the finest of all cats in the world. I wish I could give you an adequate idea of the affection that existed between us. We lived for one another. Wherever I went, Máčak followed, because of our mutual love and the desire to protect me. When such a necessity presented itself he would rise to twice his normal height, buckle his back, and with his tail as rigid as a metal bar and whiskers like steel wires, he would give vent to his rage with explosive puffs: Pfftt! Pfftt! It was a terrifying sight, and whoever had provoked him, human or animal, would beat a hasty retreat.

Every evening we would run from the house along the church wall and he would rush after me and grab me by the trousers. He tried hard to make me believe that he would bite, but the instant his needle-sharp incisors penetrated the clothing, the pressure ceased and their contact with my skin was gentle and tender as a butterfly alighting on a petal.

He liked best to roll on the grass with me. While we were doing this he bit and clawed and purred in rapturous pleasure. He fascinated me so completely that I too bit and clawed and purred. We could not stop, but rolled and rolled in a delirium of delight. We indulged in this enchanting sport day by day except in rainy weather.

In respect to water, Máčak was very fastidious. He would jump six feet to avoid wetting his paws. On such days we went into the house and selected a nice cozy place to play. Máčak was scrupulously clean, had no fleas or bugs, shed no hair, and showed no objectionable traits. He was touchingly delicate in signifying his wish to be let out at night, and scratched the door gently for readmittance.

Now I must tell you a strange and unforgettable experience that stayed with me all my life. Our home was about eighteen hundred feet above sea level, and as a rule we had dry weather in the winter. But sometimes a warm wind from the Adriatic would blow persistently for a long time, melting the snow, flooding the land, and causing great loss of property and life. We would witness the terrifying spectacle of a mighty, seething river carrying wreckage and tearing down everything moveable in its way. I often visualize the events of my youth, and when I think of this scene the sound of the waters fills my ears and I see, as vividly as then, the tumultuous flow and the mad dance of the wreckage. But my recollections of winter, with its dry cold and immaculate white snow, are always agreeable.

It happened that one day the cold was drier than ever before. People walking in the snow left a luminous trail behind them, and a snowball thrown against an obstacle gave a flare of light like a loaf of sugar cut with a knife. In the dusk of the evening, as I stroked Máčak's back, I saw a miracle that made me speechless with amazement. Máčak's back was a sheet of light and my hand produced a shower of sparks loud enough to be heard all over the house.

My father was a very learned man; he had an answer for every question. But this phenomenon was new even to him. "Well," he finally remarked, "this is nothing but electricity, the same thing you see through the trees in a storm."

My mother seemed charmed. "Stop playing with this cat," she said. "He might start a fire." But I was thinking abstractedly. Is nature a gigantic cat? If so, who strokes its back? It can only be God, I concluded. Here I was, only three years old and already philosophizing.

However stupefying the first observation, something still more wonderful was to come. It was getting darker, and soon the candles were lighted. Máčak took a few steps through the room. He shook his paws as though he were treading on wet ground. I looked at him attentively. Did I see something or was it an illusion? I strained my eyes and perceived distinctly that his body was surrounded by a halo like the aureola of a saint!

I cannot exaggerate the effect of this marvelous night on my childish imagination. Day after day I have asked myself "what is electricity?" and found no answer. Eighty years have gone by since that time and I still ask the same question, unable to answer it. Some pseudo-scientist, of whom there are only too many, may tell you that he can, but do not believe him. If any of them know what it is, I would also know, and my chances are better than any of them, for my laboratory work and practical experience are more extensive, and my life covers three generations of scientific research.

Nikola Tesla

LETTER 02

MY PRECIOUS LITTLE COMPANION IS GONE

Rachel Carson to Dorothy Freeman

18 December 1963

During Christmas of 1963, as she battled the breast cancer to which she would soon succumb, marine biologist and author Rachel Carson wrote to her dear friend, Dorothy Freeman, with some sad news: her precious cat, Jeffie, was also coming to the end of the road. A year earlier, Carson had risen to prominence with the publication of* Silent Spring*, a seminal book which helped kick-start the modern environmental movement by shining a light on the damage done by fertilisers and pesticides. That book had taken four long and stressful years to write, and Jeffie had been with her every step of the way. As Carson remarked in an earlier letter to Freeman, shortly after finishing the book:

> I took Jeffie into the study and played the Beethoven violin concerto – one of my favorites, you know. And suddenly the tensions of four years were broken and I got down and put my arms around Jeffie and let the tears come. With his little warm, rough tongue he told me that he understood.

Now, she was forced to say goodbye.

THE LETTER

Wednesday night, December 18

Dearest,

Perhaps I shouldn't write you in a minor key so close to Christmas but my heart is so burdened about Jeffie that I need to talk to you. He is slipping so fast that I feel he will surely have left us by Christmas – so much weaker each day, and now eating nothing at all but what I give him with a spoon. I was to have taken him down for a shot today but snow kept me in (I skipped my treatment too), and besides I would have hesitated about taking him out in the raw, windy cold. But if driving is possible tomorrow I guess I'll have to take him, even though I now have very little hope that anything can be done. It reminds me so much of our Tippy's last days. He was six years older than Jeffie, but I guess calendar age doesn't mean much.

You will know that deep in my heart I feel I ought to be willing and even thankful to let him go, for it would be so much easier for him to go while I am still here to care for him. You know that his fate has been one of my concerns. But it is so very hard to think of doing without him. His little life has been so intertwined with mine all these ten years. And how strange it would be if the three darling kitties that have meant so much to you and to us should all die within the year!

Now it is Thursday morning and my precious little companion is gone. I imagine I shall have talked to you before this reaches you and you will know. I sat up late with him in the living room, then carried him into the bedroom and closed the door so I could check on him more easily during the night. About 3:30 I was wakened by the sound of his difficult breathing, with little moans, and found him lying at the door. I sat on the floor beside him for some time, stroking him and talking to him. Finally he got up and went under the bed. That is where he died this morning, I think just before Roger left for school. We both heard him cry just as we finished breakfast. We came in and Roger reported he was under the bed. I could not see him well, but after Roger left I got down with a flash light and then I knew. In a few minutes Ida came, and she moved the bed so I could lift him out and hold him in my arms. Then we curled him up in the little battered oval basket he loved so well. I will have Elliott bury him out under the pine trees by the study, a place that I should think would never be disturbed.

So many sad and somber thoughts, which I should not even try to express. For exactly three years, since I flew to Cleveland in December and first understood my own situation, I have worried about my little family. I knew no one could take care of Jeffie, and I felt it unlikely that whoever takes Roger would want to adopt a cat, too, so even Moppet was a problem. Last September when she died I felt that the inevitable dissolution of my little circle had begun. Now I have lived to witness another step. But oh, I should be glad for Jeffie, and soon I know I can be, for it would have been awful for him, and so frightening, if he had survived me. Now that problem exists no more.

Darling, I suppose I oughtn't to send you such thoughts, but it seems I have to express them.

Now this means Roger and I can come to you, leaving, and returning to, such a strangely empty house. I'll discuss with you the best time. Now that it makes no difference here, I am wondering whether morning or evening is the easiest time for you to meet the train, in terms of weather. Of course we won't go at a time we know the weather will be bad.

I have to go down for a treatment this afternoon. It's cold and windy, but bright, and I guess most of the snow is off the roads. I'll be talking to you tonight if you're home, dear. Meanwhile, all my love.

Rachel

LETTER 03
THE CAT RANCH

Jack Lemmon to Walter Matthau

23 December 1988

Jack Lemmon and Walter Matthau shared the screen many times during their Hollywood careers, most notably in *The Odd Couple* ***in 1968 and, twenty-five years later, in*** *Grumpy Old Men*, ***both comedies that benefited enormously from an on-screen chemistry rarely witnessed. Off-screen, perhaps unsurprisingly, they were the best of friends, and shared a mischievous sense of humour that spilled over into their correspondence. Over the course of their relationship they sent each other countless witty letters in an effort to raise a laugh. In December of 1988, as Christmas approached, Lemmon put pen to paper and revived an old gag that was first spotted in an Illinois newspaper in 1875.***

THE LETTER

December 23rd, 1988

Mr. Walter Matthau
278 Toyopa
Pacific Palisades
California 90272

Dear Waltz:
I know you're always interested in looking for opportunities for investment.

I don't know if you would be interested in this, but I thought I would mention it to you because it could be a real "sleeper" in making a lot of money with very little investment.

A group of us are considering investing in a large cat ranch near Hermosillo, Mexico. It is our purpose to start rather small, with about one million cats. Each cat averages about twelve kittens a year: skins can be sold for about 20¢ for the white ones and up to 40¢ for the black. This will give us 12 million cat skins per year to sell at an average price of around 32¢, making our revenues about $3 million a year. This really averages out to £10 thousand a day – excluding Sundays and holidays.

A good Mexican cat man can skin about 50 cats per day at a wage of $3.15 a day. It will only take 663 men to operate the ranch so the net profit would be over $8,200 per day.

Now, the cats would be fed on rats exclusively. Rats multiply four times as fast as cats. We would start a ranch adjacent to our cat farm. If we start with a million rats, we will have four rats per cat each day. The rats will be fed on the carcasses of the cats that we skin. This will give each rat a quarter of a cat. You can see by this that this business is a clean operation – self-supporting and really automatic throughout. The cats will eat the rats and the rats will eat the cats and we will get the skins.

Let me know if you are interested. As you can imagine, I am rather particular who I want to get into this, and want the fewest investors possible.

Eventually, it is my hope to cross the cats with snakes, for they will skin themselves twice a year. This would save labor costs of skinning as well as give me two skins for one cat.

I really felt that giving you an opportunity like this would be the greatest Christmas present possible.

Love,

Jack

‘IT IS OUR PURPOSE TO
START RATHER SMALL,
WITH ABOUT ONE
MILLION CATS.’

– *Jack Lemmon*

LETTER 04
MY FLUTTERING HEART

Persian Snow (Erasmus Darwin) and Miss Po Felina (Anna Seward)

September 1780

When first published in 1804, poet Anna Seward's *Memoirs of the Life of Dr. Darwin* ***– a biography of English physician and philosopher Erasmus Darwin, who had died in 1802 and was grandfather to Charles Darwin – raised more than a few eyebrows, and indeed anger from his family, due to the unexpected inclusion of this curious exchange of correspondence: in 1780 it seems Darwin had sent to Seward, whom he had known for many years, a playful and quite suggestive love letter that was addressed to her cat, Miss Po Felina, written in the voice of*** *his* ***cat, Persian Snow. Naturally, her cat responded, and in the memoir both sides of the exchange were reproduced. If nothing else, the letters revealed a fascinating, otherwise unseen side to Darwin, and at the time served to generate much debate about the relationship between biographer and subject. The cats themselves escaped with their reputations unscathed.***

THE LETTERS

Lichfield Vicarage,
Sept. 7th. 1780.

Dear Miss Pussey,
As I sat, the other day, basking myself in the Dean's Walk, I saw you, in your stately palace, washing your beautiful round face, and elegantly brinded ears, with your velvet paws, and whisking about, with graceful sinuosity, your meandering tail. That treacherous hedgehog, Cupid, concealed himself behind your tabby beauties, and darting one of his too well aimed quills, pierced, O cruel imp! my fluttering heart.

Ever since that fatal hour have I watched, day and night, in my balcony, hoping that the stillness of the starlight evenings might induce you to take the air on the leads of the palace. Many serenades have I sung under you windows; and, when you failed to appear, with the sound of my voice made the vicarage re-echo through all its winding lanes and dirty alleys. All heard me but my cruel Fair-one; she, wrapped in fur, sat purring with contented insensibility, or slept with untroubled dreams.

Though I cannot boast those delicate varieties of melody with which you sometimes ravish the ear of night, and stay the listening stars; though you sleep hourly on the lap of the favourite of the muses, and are patted by those fingers which hold the pen of science; and every day, with her permission, dip your white whiskers in delicious cream; yet am I not destitute of all advantages of birth, education, and beauty. Derived from Persian kings, my snowy fur yet retains the whiteness and splendour of their ermine.

This morning, as I sat up on the Doctor's tea-table, and saw my reflected features in the slop-basin, my long white whiskers, ivory teeth, and topaz eyes, I felt an agreeable presentiment of my suit; and certainly the slop-basin did not flatter me, which shews the azure flowers upon its borders less beauteous than they are.

You know not, dear Miss Pussey Po, the value of the address you neglect. New milk have I, in flowing abundance, and mice pent up in twenty garrets, for your food and amusement.

Permit me, this afternoon, to lay at your divine feet the head of an enormous Norway rat, which has even now stained my paws with its gore. If you will do me the honour to sing the following song, which I have taken the liberty to write, as expressing the sentiments I wish you to entertain, I will bring a band of catgut and catcall, to accompany you in chorus.

Air: – *spirituosi*.

Cats I scorn, who, sleek and fat,
Shiver at a Norway rat;
Rough and hardy, bold and free,
Be the cat that's made for me!
He, whose nervous paw can take
My lady's lapdog by the neck;
With furious hiss attack the hen,
And snatch the chicken from the pen.
If the treacherous swain should prove
Rebellious to my tender love,
My scorn the vengeful paw shall dart,
Shall tear his fur, and pierce his heart.

Chorus:

Qu-ow wow, quall, wawl, moon.

Deign, most adorable charmer, to purr your assent to this my request, and believe me to be with the profoundest respect, your true admirer,

Snow

Miss Seward's answer:

Palace, Lichfield.
Sept. 8th. 1780.

I am but too sensible of the charms of Mr. Snow; but while I admire the spotless whiteness of his ermine, and the tyger-strength of his commanding form, I sigh in secret, that he, who sucked the milk of benevolence and philosophy, should yet retain the extreme of the fierceness, too justly imputed to the Grimalkin race. Our hereditary violence is perhaps commendable when we exert it against the foes of our protectors, but deserves much blame when it annoys their friends.

The happiness of a refined education was mine; yet, dear Mr. Snow, my advantages in that respect were not equal to what yours might have been; but, while you give unbounded indulgence to your carnivorous desires, I have so far subdued mine, that the lark pours his mattin song, the canary bird warbles wild and loud, and the robin pipes his farewell song to the setting sun, unmolested in my presence; nay, the plump and tempting dove has reposed securely on my soft back, and bent her glossy neck in graceful curves as she walked round me.

But let me hasten to tell thee how my sensibilities in thy favour were, last month, unfortunately repressed. Once, in the noon of one of its most beautiful nights, I was invited abroad by the serenity of the amorous hour, secretly stimulated by the hope of meeting my admired Persian. With silent steps I paced around the dimly gleaming leads of the palace. I had acquired a taste for scenic beauty and poetic imagery, by listening to ingenious observations upon their nature from the lips of thy own lord, as I lay purring at the feet of my mistress.

I admired the lovely scene, and breathed my sighs for thee to the listening moon. She threw the long shadows of the majestic cathedral upon the silvered lawn. I beheld the pearly meadows of Stow Valley, and the lake in its bosom, which, reflecting the lunar rays, seemed a sheet of diamonds. The trees of the Dean's Walk, which the hand of Dulness had been restrained from torturing into trim and detestable regularity, met each other in a thousand various and beautiful forms. Their liberated boughs danced on the midnight gale, and the edges of their leaves were whitened by the moonbeams. I descended to the lawn, that I might throw the beauties of the valley into perspective through the graceful arches, formed by their meeting branches. Suddenly my ear was startled, not by the voice of my lover, but by the loud and dissonant noise of the war-song, which six black grimalkins were raising in honour of the numerous victories obtained by the Persian, Snow; compared with which, they acknowledged those of English cats had little brilliance, eclipsed, like the unimportant victories of the Howes, by the puissant Clinton and Arbuthnot, and the still more puissant Cornwallis. It sung that thou didst owe thy matchless might to thy lineal descent from the invincible Alexander, as he derived his more than mortal valour from his mother Olympia's illicit commerce with Jupiter. They sang that, amid the renowned siege of Persepolis, while Roxana and Statira were contending for the honour of his attentions, the conqueror of the world deigned to bestow them upon a large, white female cat, thy grandmother, warlike Mr. Snow, in the ten thousandth and ninety-ninth ascent.

Thus far their triumphant din was music to my ear; and even when it sung that lakes of milk ran curdling into whey, within the ebon concave of their pancheons, with terror at thine approach; that mice squealed from all the neighbouring garrets; and that whole armies of Norway rats, crying out amain, "the devil take the hindmost", ran violently into the minster-pool, at the first gleam of thy white mail through the shrubs of Mr. Howard's garden.

But O! when they sang, or rather yelled, of larks

warbling on sunbeams, fascinated suddenly by the glare of thine eyes, and falling into thy remorseless talons; of robins, warbling soft and solitary upon the leafless branch, till the pale cheek of winter dimpled into joy; of hundreds of those bright breasted songsters, torn from their barren sprays by thy pitiless fangs! – Alas! my heart died within me at the idea of so preposterous a union!

Marry you, Mr. Snow, I'm afraid I cannot; since, though the laws of our community might not oppose our connection, yet those of principle, of delicacy, of duty to my mistress, do very powerfully oppose it.

As to presiding at your concert, if you extremely wish it, I may perhaps grant your request; but then you must allow me to sing a song of my own composition, applicable to our present situation, and set to music by my sister Sophy at Mr. Brown's the organist's, thus,

Air: – *affettuoso*.
He, whom Pussy Po detains
A captive in her silken chains,
Must curb the furious thirst of prey,
Nor rend the warbler from his spray!
Nor let his wild, ungenerous rage
An unprotected foe engage.
O, should cat of Darwin prove

Foe to pity, foe to love!
Cat, that listens day by day,
To mercy's mild and honied lay,
Too surely would the dire disgrace
More deeply brand our future race,
The stigma fix, where'er they range,
That cats can ne'er their nature change.

Should I content with thee to wed,
These sanguine crimes upon thy head,
And ere the wish'd reform I see,
Adieu to lapping Seward's tea!
Adieu to purring gentle praise
Charm'd as she quotes thy master's lays!
Could I, alas! our kittens bring
Where sweet her plumy favorites sing,
Would not the watchful nymph espy
Their father's fierceness in their eye.
And drive us far and wide away,
In cold and lonely barn to stray?
Where the dark owl, with hideous scream,
Shall mock our yells for forfeit cream,
As on starv'd mice we swearing dine
And grumble that our lives are nine.

Chorus: – *largo.*
Waal, woee, trone, moan, mall, oll, moule.

The still too much admired Mr. Snow will have the goodness to pardon the freedom of these expostulations and excuse their imperfections. The morning, O Snow! had been devoted to this my correspondence with thee, but I was interrupted in that employment by the visit of two females of our species, who fed my ill-starred passion by praising thy wit and endowments, exemplified by thy elegant letter, to which the delicacy of my sentiments obliges me to send so inauspicious a reply.

I am, dear Mr. Snow,

Your ever obliged

Po Felina

LETTER 05
A HUMAN CARESS FROM A CAT

Sylvia Townsend Warner and David Garnett

June 1973

Sylvia Townsend Warner first met David Garnett in 1922, in the London bookshop in which he worked – she was twenty-nine, he was a year older. They had much in common, particularly in the literary sense, and clicked instantly, their ensuing friendship lasting until Warner passed away fifty-six years later, by which point they had both become celebrated novelists. They wrote to each other hundreds of times over the years, on all manner of subjects, their gentle letters glowing with a mutual affection. In June of 1973 they exchanged letters on the subject of cats.

THE LETTERS

Dearest Sylvia,
Can you explain how and why cats make love to us? Tiber will come, if I am reading or writing or lying on my bed and will "tease tow" with his claws. Then coming closer, will gaze into my face, suddenly dig his pointed muzzle under my chin once or twice, retreat, roll on his side, inviting my hand, turn his head dreamily to one side, passive and luxurious. Then he will turn on me almost fiercely with a burst of purring, and so on, and so on.

But is this, as I think, reserved for human lovers? With a female cat I think he displays no such graces but is fiercely practical. It is more like the love that was shown him by his mother when he was a kitten. And naturally it is shown most strongly before and after I have fed him. But the luxury of his furry love is very beautiful.

He fights continually with the Wood Cat–a savage beast that has run wild and supports himself in the wood by hunting, flying from man. He is more versed in battle, and Tiber is continually appearing with his scalp furrowed by the Wood Cat's claws, paws bitten through and lame, ears bleeding. He has just recovered after some days of lameness when his paw was swollen like a boxing-glove. I keep him shut up at night to save further fights, but now he can put his paw to the ground he will go off to fight again.

We had a terrible storm yesterday evening, with all the artillery of Heaven and hailstones like large lumps of sugar bouncing all over the carpet from the chimney, and today the leaves are torn and many barley fields laid flat and peasants half ruined. Every room was flooded–except the bathroom.

Very much love from

David

* * *

Dearest David,

Tiber makes love to you for the good reason that he loves you, and loves making love. Cats are passionate and voluptuous, they get satisfaction from mating but no pleasure (the females dislike it, and this is wounding to the male), no voluptuousness; and no appreciation. Tiber has the pleasure of being pleased and knowing he pleases in his love-making with you. I am so glad you have each other. Does he roll on his head? Does he fall asleep with an ownerly paw laid over you?

We had a dark grey cat (Norfolk bred, very

Norfolk in character) called Tom. He was reserved, domineering, voluptuous–much as I imagine Tiber to be. When he was middle-aged he gave up nocturnal prowlings and slept on my bed, against my feet. One evening I was reading in bed when I became aware that Tom was staring at me. I put down my book, said nothing, watched. Slowly, with a look of intense concentration, he got up and advanced on me, like Tarquin with ravishing strides, poised himself, put out a front paw, and stroked my cheek as I used to stroke his chops. A human caress from a cat. I felt very meagre and ill-educated that I could not purr.

It had never occurred to me that their furry love develops from what was shown them as kittens. I expect you are right. The ownerly paw is certainly a nursing cat's gesture.

You should encourage Tiber to sleep with you. He might come to prefer it to midnight battling with the Wood Cat. Come winter, he certainly will. I am afraid of the Wood Cat's claws, still more of his teeth.

Were your hailstones blue? We once had such a storm here, with lightning ripping hail from the sky; and the hailstones were hard as marbles, and blue as aquamarines. And there was another storm, after a long drought, when the lightning was green. It was strange to see the bleached fields, the rusty trees, momentarily sluiced with the look of spring.

I have been spared acquaintances who might have explained to me about blue hailstones and green lightning, so I can enjoy them with simple pleasure.

> Earth that grew with joyful ease
> Hemlock for Socrates–

The longer I live, the more my heart assents to that couplet.

With love,
Sylvia

LETTER 06
YOU KILLED MY CAT

Guy Davenport to the drivers of Lexington:

Date unknown

Born in South Carolina in 1927, Guy Davenport was many things: a writer of fiction; an illustrator, sometimes of his own stories; a painter; a published poet; an award-winning translator of ancient Greek texts; a critic; and a Professor of English. He also, most importantly, loved his cat, and when his beloved feline friend was run over on the streets of Lexington, Kentucky, Davenport reacted by writing a furious letter addressed to the drivers of his city. He then sent that letter to the popular *Lexington Herald* ***newspaper and paid for it to be printed in its pages.***

THE LETTER

TO THE DRIVERS OF LEXINGTON:
All of you, without exception, gape-mouthed teenagers who squawl your tires around the clock with no policeman to say you nay, ministers of God who take time off from sliding around in your Mercedes-Benzes to set me an example of charity, blue-haired ladies who never in your life have seen a stop sign, politicians too terrified of losing a vote to do anything about traffic which defines anarchy and illustrates idiocy, speeders, light-jumpers, drunks, dope-addicts, and the entire moronic, arrogant, shiftless lot of you: you have killed some 900 of yourselves this year in Kentucky, and maimed another 2000 for life, and this afternoon you killed my cat – not, I'm certain, on purpose, for with yourselves to kill, and children, and bigger game than cats, I do not suppose you could focus your feeble wits enough to do anything as concentrated as a deliberate act. You killed my cat out of the same sloth and God-forsaken laziness and pride by which you use the city streets for a race track and a parade ground to show off all that you have of significance on this earth, your expensive, poisonous, noisy, bullying, fast, lethal automobiles. I have taken this ad to express openly my utter

contempt for the lot of you, and for the politicians who pretend to govern our city and who still let you have your selfish and degraded pleasure behind the wheel.

Sincerely,

Guy Davenport

LETTER 07
LONG TAILS DANCING AT NIGHT

Lafcadio Hearn to Basil Hall Chamberlain

August 1891

In 1890, after twenty years in the US where he was known for his extensive writings on New Orleans, Greek-born author Lafcadio Hearn moved to Japan and immediately fell in love with a culture and language about which he would write, in books and in letters, until his death fourteen years later. In 1891, having lived in Japan for a year, Hearn, also a great lover of cats, wrote this letter to his friend Basil Hall Chamberlain, a British-born Japanologist and professor of Japanese in Tokyo who had moved to Japan in 1873.

THE LETTER

Matsue, August, 1891.

Dear Professor Chamberlain,–
Having reached a spot where I can write upon something better than a matted floor, I find three most pleasant letters from you. The whole of the questions in them I cannot answer to-night, but will do so presently, when I obtain the full information.

However, as to cats' tails I can answer at once. Izumo cats – (and I was under the impression until recently that all Japanese cats were alike) – are generally born with long tails. But there is a belief that any cat whose tail is not cut off in kittenhood, will become an *obake* [a ghost] or a *nekomata* [a supernatural, double-tailed], and there are weird stories about cats with long tails dancing at night, with towels tied round their heads. There are stories about petted cats eating their mistress and then assuming the form, features, and voice of the victim. Of course you know the Buddhist tradition that no cat can enter paradise. The cat and the snake alone wept not for the death of Buddha. Cats are unpopular in Izumo, but in Hōki I saw that they seemed to exist under more favourable conditions. The real reason for the unpopularity of the cat is its powers of mischief in a Japanese house;– it tears the *tatami* [floor mat], the *karakami* [decorative paper], the *shoji* [sliding door], scratches the woodwork, and insists upon carrying its food into the best room to eat it upon the floor. I am a great lover of cats, having "raised," as the Americans say, more than fifty;– but I could not gratify my desire to have a cat here. The creature proved too mischievous, and wanted always to eat my uguisu.

The oscillation of one's thoughts concerning the Japanese – the swaying you describe – is and has for some time been mine also.

There are times when they seem so small! And then again, although they never seem large, there is a vastness behind them, – a past of indefinite complexity and marvel, – an amazing power of absorbing and assimilating, – which forces one to suspect some power in the race so different from our own that one cannot understand that power. And as you say, whatever doubts or vexations one has in Japan, it is only necessary to ask one's self:– "Well, who are the best people to live with?" For it is a question whether the intellectual pleasures of social life abroad are not more than dearly bought at the cost of social pettinesses which do not seem to exist in Japan at all.

[. . .]

As usual, I find I have been too presumptuous in writing offhand about cats' tails. On enquiring, I learn that there are often, born of the same mother, Izumo kittens with short tails, and kittens with long tails. This would show that two distinct species of cats exist here. The long-tailed kittens are always deprived when possible of the larger part of their caudal appendage. The short tails are spared. If an old cat be seen with a short tail, people say, – "this cat is old, but she has a short tail: therefore she is a good cat." (For the obake cat gets two tails when old, and every wicked cat has a long tail.) I am told that at the recent bon, in Matsue, cats of the evil sort were seen to dance upon the roofs of the houses.

What you tell me about those Shintō rituals and their suspicious origin seems to me quite certainly true. So the kara-shishi and the mon and the dragon-carvings and the tōrōs, – all stare me in the face as pillage of Buddhism. But the funeral rite which I saw and took part in, on the anniversary of the death of Prince Sanjō, struck me as immemorially primitive. The weird simplicity of it – the banquet to the ghost, the covering of the faces with white paper, the moaning song, the barbarian music, all seemed to me traditions and echoes of the very childhood of the race. I shall try to discover the genesis of the book you speak of as dubious in character. The Shintō christening ceremony is strictly observed here, and there are curious facts about the funeral ceremonies – totally at variance with and hostile to Buddhism.

By the way, when I visited a tera [Buddhist temple] in Mionoseki after having bought o fuda [amulet] at the Miojinja, I was told I must not carry the o fuda into the court of the tera. The Kami would be displeased.

For the moment, good-bye.

Ever faithfully,

Lafcadio Hearn

LETTER 08
POOR MOUSCHI!

Anne Frank to Kitty

10 May 1944

In July of 1942, shortly after her sister, Margot, received a letter from the Nazis demanding that she attend a German labour camp, thirteen-year-old Jewish girl Anne Frank went into hiding with her family in Amsterdam. For the next two years the Franks lived above offices belonging to Otto, Anne's father, and it was during this period that Anne documented her family's struggle by writing letters in her now-famous diary – all addressed to Kitty, a character from a series of novels Anne liked. In May of 1944, three months before her family were captured by the Gestapo, Anne wrote to Kitty with news of an incident involving Mouschi, a tabby cat belonging to Peter van Pels, the son of Otto's colleague, who was also in hiding. Within a year of this particular letter being written, Anne and Margot Frank had died in Bergen-Belsen concentration camp.

THE LETTER

Wednesday, 10 May, 1944

Dearest Kitty,

We were sitting in the attic yesterday afternoon working on our French when suddenly I heard the splatter of water behind me. I asked Peter what it might be. Without pausing to reply, he dashed up to the loft – the scene of the disaster – and shoved Mouschi, who was squatting beside her soggy litter box, back to the right place. This was followed by shouts and squeals, and then Mouschi, who by that time had finished peeing, took off downstairs. In search of something similar to her box, Mouschi had found herself a pile of wood shavings, right over a crack in the floor. The puddle immediately trickled down to the attic and, as luck would have it, landed in and next to the potato barrel. The ceiling was dripping, and since the attic floor has also got its share of cracks, little yellow drops were leaking through the ceiling and onto the dining table, between a pile of stockings and books.

I was doubled up with laughter, it was such a funny sight. There was Mouschi crouched under a chair, Peter armed with water, powdered bleach and a cloth, and Mr. van Daan trying to calm everyone down. The room was soon set to rights, but it's a well-known fact that cat puddles stink to high heaven. The potatoes proved that all too well, as did the wood shavings, which Father collected in a bucket and brought downstairs to burn.

Poor Mouschi! How were you to know it's impossible to get peat for your box?

Anne

LETTER 09

IT IS LIKE LIVING IN A STATE OF SIEGE

Charles Dickens to John Forster

6 July 1856

During the summer of 1851, while the family were holidaying at Fort House on the coast of Broadstairs, Kent, the daughters of Charles Dickens were given a young canary, just a few weeks old, by a local lady who reared birds. Dick, as they called him, was adored by all, and settled in quickly, soon becoming one of the family. He began to attract attention from two cats who loitered to the rear of the house. Dickens described the situation in a letter to his friend and biographer, John Forster. Thankfully, Dick lived for another decade, and was buried beneath a rose tree at Gad's Hill Place, Higham, on 14 October 1866. The surviving cats eventually gave up, never to be seen again.

THE LETTER

6th July 1856

The only thing new in this garden is that war is raging against two particularly tigerish and fearful cats (from the mill, I suppose), which are always glaring in dark corners, after our wonderful little Dick. Keeping the house open at all points, it is impossible to shut them out, and they hide themselves in the most terrific manner: hanging themselves up behind draperies, like bats, and tumbling out in the dead of night with frightful caterwaulings. Hereupon, French borrows Beaucourt's gun, loads the same to the muzzle, discharges it twice in vain and throws himself over with the recoil, exactly like a clown. But at last (while I was in town) he aims at the more amiable cat of the two, and shoots that animal dead. Insufferably elated by this victory, he is now engaged from morning to night in hiding behind bushes to get aim at the other. He does nothing else whatever. All the boys encourage him and watch for the enemy – on whose appearance they give an alarm which immediately serves as a warning to the creature, who runs away. They are at this moment (ready dressed for church) all lying on their stomachs in various parts of the garden. Horrible whistles give notice to the gun what point it is to approach. I am afraid to go out, lest I should be shot. Mr. Plornish says his prayers at night in a whisper, lest the cat should overhear him and take offence. The tradesmen cry out as they come up the avenue, 'Me voici! C'est moi – boulanger – ne tirez pas, Monsieur Franche!' It is like living in a state of siege; and the wonderful manner in which the cat preserves the character of being the only person not much put out by the intensity of this monomania, is most ridiculous. About four pounds of powder and half a ton of shot have been (13th of July) fired off at the cat (and the public in general) during the week. The finest thing is that immediately after I have the noble sportsman blazing away at her in the garden in front, I look out of my room door into the drawing-room and am pretty sure to see her coming in after the bird, in the calmest manner possible, by the back window.

‘WAR IS RAGING
AGAINST TWO
PARTICULARLY
TIGERISH AND
FEARFUL CATS.’

– *Charles Dickens*

LETTER 10
TO ALL POLLICLE DOGS & JELLICLE CATS

T.S. Eliot to Thomas Faber

1931

In 1931, eight years prior to the publication of his much-loved collection of poems, *Old Possum's Book of Practical Cats,* ***American poet and publisher T.S. Eliot wrote to his godson, Thomas Faber, on the occasion of his fourth birthday. This letter, and the delightful spoof party invitation it contained, would eventually inspire Eliot's aforementioned book, which in turn, decades later, would be adapted to become the phenomenally successful Andrew Lloyd Webber musical,*** *Cats.* ***Eliot corresponded with Thomas until Eliot passed away in 1965.***

THE LETTER

FABER & FABER
Limited
PUBLISHERS
24 RUSSELL SQUARE
LONDON, W.C.1
Easter 1931.

Dear Tom,
I Believe that your are to have a Birthday soon, and I think that you will then be Four Years Old (I am not Clever at Arithmetic) but that is a Great Age, so I thought we might send out this

INVITATION
TO ALL POLLICLE DOGS & JELLICLE CATS
TO COME TO THE BIRTHDAY OF
THOMAS FABER.

Pollicle Dogs and Jellicle Cats!
Come from your Kennels & Houses & Flats;
Pollicle Dogs & Cats, draw near;
Jellicle Cats & Dogs, Appear;
Come with your Ears & your Whiskers & Tails
Over the Mountains & Valleys of Wales.
This is your ONLY CHANCE THIS YEAR,
Your ONLY CHANCE to – what do you spose? –

Brush Up your Coats and Turn out your Toes,
And come with a Hop & a Skip & a Dance –
Because, for this year, it's your ONLY CHANCE
To come with your Whiskers & Tails & Hair on
To
Ty Glyn Aeron
Ciliau Aeron –
Because your are INVITED to Come
With a Flute & a Fife & a Fiddle & Drum,
With a Fiddle, a Fife, & a Drum & a Tabor
(A Musicle Instrument that makes a Joyful Noise)
To the Birthday Party of
THOMAS ERLE FABER!

Oh But P.S. we mustn't send out this Invitation after All, Because, if ALL the Pollicle Dogs & Jellicle Cats came (and of course they would come) then all the roads would be blocked up, and what's more, they would track Muddy Feet into the House, and your Mother wouldn't Like that at All, and what's More Still, you would have to give them All a Piece of your Birthday Cake, and there would be so Many that there wouldn't be any Cake left for you, and that would be Dreadful, so we won't send out this Invitation, so no more for the Present from your Silly Uncle

Tom

LETTER 11
I SEE YOU, MY BEAUTY BOY

Elizabeth Taylor to her missing cat

1974

For two months in 1974, as Welsh movie star Richard Burton filmed his part in *The Klansman* ***alongside Lee Marvin and O. J. Simpson, he and Elizabeth Taylor, to whom he was married, moved to California with Cassius, just one of Taylor's many beloved cats. Confused by his new surroundings, Cassius soon went missing from their rented home, leaving Taylor distraught. Before long, having tried everything to locate her precious feline friend, Taylor wrote him a letter. Sadly, Cassius never returned. To make matters worse, the stress of the move resulted in Taylor and Burton's divorce on their return home. They remarried the next year.***

THE LETTER

Letter to my Lovely Lost Cat

I see you, my beauty boy, in the reflection of those shining black-brown rocks ahead of me. I see the green o' thy eyes in every rained, sweated leaf shaking in my eyes.

I remember the sweet smell of your fur against my neck when I was deeply in trouble and how, somehow you made it better – you knew! You knew always when I hurt and you made comfort for me, as I did once for you when you were a broken kitten.

Anyway, I love you Cassius – and thank you for your beauty.

Please come back!

LETTER 12
THE CAT IS NOT A SIMPLE EQUATION

Henry Harland to *The Yellow Book*

July 1896

Born in Brooklyn in 1861, Henry Harland spent the first part of his career writing a commercially successful but critically knocked series of stories about Jewish life in the US using the pseudonym Sidney Luska, who most people believed to be a Jewish immigrant. In 1889 he moved to London, dropped the disguise, and with his real name on show began writing novels that garnered critical acclaim. In 1894 Harland also became literary editor of* The Yellow Book*, an English quarterly that ran for three years and for which Harland sometimes also wrote, alongside names such as Henry James and W.B. Yeats. It was in* The Yellow Book*, in 1896, that this letter appeared, written by 'The Yellow Dwarf', a regular contributor to the periodical who later turned out to be Harland.

THE LETTER

Sir,

I hope you will not suspect me of making a bid for his affection, when I remark that the Average Man loves the Obvious. By consequence (for, like all unthinking creatures, the duffer's logical), by consequence, his attitude towards the Subtle, the Elusive, when not an attitude of mere torpid indifference, is an attitude of positive distrust and dislike.

Of this ignoble fact, pretty nearly everything – from the popularity of beer and skittles, to the popularity of Mr. Hall Caine's novels; from the general's distaste for caviare, to the general's neglect of Mr. Henry James's tales – pretty nearly everything is a reminder. But, to go no further afield, for the moment, than his own hearthrug, may I ask you to consider a little the relative positions occupied in the Average Man's regard by the Dog and the Cat?

The Average Man ostentatiously loves the Dog.

The Average Man, when he is not torpidly indifferent to that princely animal, positively distrusts and dislikes the Cat.

I have used the epithet "princely" with intention, in speaking of the near relative of the King of Beasts. The Cat is a Princess of the Blood. Yes, my dear, always a Princess, though the Average Man, with his unerring instinct for the malappropriate word, sometimes names her Thomas. The Cat is always a Princess, because everything nice in this world, everything fine, sensitive, distinguished, everything beautiful, everything worth while, is of essence Feminine, though it may be male by the accident of sex;– and that's as true as gospel, let Mr. W. E. Henley's lusty young disciples shout their loudest in celebration of the Virile. – The Cat is a Princess.

The Dog, on the contrary, is not even a gentleman. Far otherwise. His admirers may do what they will to forget it, the circumstance remains, writ large in every Natural History, that the Dog is sprung from quite the meanest family of the Quadrupeds. That coward thief the wolf is his bastard brother; the carrion hyena is his cousin-german. And in his person, as in his character, bears he not an hundred marks of his base descent? In his rough coat (contrast it with the silken mantle of the Cat); in his harsh, monotonous voice (contrast it with the flexible organ of the Cat, her versatile mewings, chirrupings, and purrings, and their innumerable shades and modulations); in the stiff-jointed clumsiness of his movements (compare them to the inexpressible grace and suppleness of the Cat's); briefly, in the all-pervading plebeian commonness that hangs about him like an atmosphere (compare it to the high-bred reserve and dignity that invest the Cat). The wolf's brother, is the Dog not himself a coward? Watch him when, emulating the ruffian who insults an unprotected lady, he puts a Cat to flight in the streets: watch him when the lady halts and turns. Faugh, the craven! with his wild show of savagery so long as there is not the slightest danger – and his sudden chopfallen drawing back when the lady halts and turns! The hyena's cousin, is he not himself of carrion an impassioned amateur? At Constantinople he serves ('tis a labour of love; he receives no stipend) he serves as Public Scavenger, swallowing with greed the ordures cast by the Turk. Scripture tells us to what he returneth: who has failed to observe that he returneth not to his own alone? And the other day, strolling upon the sands by the illimitable sea, I came upon a friend and her pet terrier. She was holding the little beggar by the scruff of his neck, and giving him repeated sousings in a pool. I stood a pleased spectator of this exercise, for the terrier kicked and spluttered and appeared to be unhappy. "He found a decaying jelly-fish below there, and rolled in it," my friend pathetically explained. I should like to see the Cat who could be induced to roll in a decaying jelly-fish. The Cat's fastidiousness, her meticulous cleanliness, the time and the pains she bestows upon her toilet, and her almost morbid delicacy about certain more private errands, are among the material indications of her patrician nature. It were needless to allude to the vile habits and impudicity of the Dog.

Have you ever met a Dog who wasn't a bounder? Have you ever met a Dog who wasn't a bully, a sycophant, and a snob? Have you ever met a Cat who was? Have you ever met a Cat who would half frighten a timid little girl to death, by rushing at her and barking? Have you ever met a Cat who, left alone with a visitor in your drawing-room, would truculently growl and show her teeth, as often as that visitor ventured to stir in his chair? Have you ever met a Cat who would snarl and snap at the servants, Mawster's back being turned? Have you ever met a Cat who would cringe to you and fawn to you, and kiss the hand that smote her?

Conscious of her high lineage, the Cat understands and accepts the responsibilities that attach to it. She knows what she owes to herself, to her rank, to the Royal Idea. Therefore, it is you who must be the courtier. The Dog, poor-spirited toady, will study your eye to divine your mood, and slavishly adapt his own mood and his behaviour to it. Not so the Cat. As between you and her, it is you who must do the toadying. A guest in the house, never a dependent, she remembers always the courtesy and the consideration that are her due. You must respect her pleasure. Is it her pleasure to slumber, and do you disturb her: note the disdainful melancholy with which she silently comments your rudeness. Is it her pleasure to be grave: tempt her to frolic, you will tempt in vain. Is it her pleasure to be cold: nothing in human possibility can win a caress from her. Is it her pleasure to be rid of your presence: only the physical influence of a closed door will persuade her to remain in the room with you. It is you who must be the courtier, and wait upon her desire.

But then!

When, in her own good time, she chooses to unbend, how graciously, how entrancingly, she does it! Oh, the thousand wonderful lovelinesses and surprises of her play! The wit, the humour, the imagination, that inform it! Her ruses, her false leads, her sudden triumphs, her feigned despairs! And the topazes and emeralds that sparkle in her eyes; the satiny lustre of her apparel; the delicious sinuosities of her body! And her parenthetic interruptions of the game: to stride in regal progress round the apartment, flourishing her tail like a banner: or coquettishly to throw herself in some enravishing posture at length upon the carpet at your feet: or (if she loves you) to leap upon your shoulder, and press her cheek to yours, and murmur rapturous assurances of her passion! To be loved by a Princess! Whosoever, from the Marquis de Carabas down, has been loved by a Cat, has savoured that felicity. My own particular treasure of a Cat, at this particular moment is lying wreathed about my neck, watching my pen as it moves along the paper, and purring approbation of my views. But when, from time to time, I chance to use a word that doesn't strike her altogether as the fittest, she reaches down her little velvet paw, and dabs it out. I should like to see the Dog who could do that.

But – the Cat is subtle, the Cat is elusive, the Cat is not to be read at a glance, the Cat is not a simple equation. And so the Average Man, gross mutton-devouring, money-grubbing mechanism that he is, when he doesn't just torpidly tolerate her, distrusts her and dislikes her. A great soul, misappreciated, misunderstood, she sits neglected in his chimney-corner; and the fatuous idgit never guesses how she scorns him.

But – the Dog is obvious. Any fool can grasp the meaning of the Dog. And the Average Man, accordingly, recreant for once to the snobbism which is his religion, hugs the hyena's cousin to his bosom.

What of it?

Only this: that in the Average Man's sentimental

attitude towards the Dog and the Cat, we have a formula, a symbol, for his sentimental attitude towards many things, especially for his sentimental attitude towards Books.

Some books, in their uncouthness, their awkwardness, their boisterousness, in their violation of the decencies of art, in their low truckling to the tastes of the purchaser, in their commonness, their vulgarity, in their total lack of suppleness and distinction, are the very Dogs of Bookland. The Average Man loves 'em.

Such as they are, they're obvious.

And other books, by reason of their beauties and their virtues, their graces and refinements; because they are considered finished; because they are delicate, distinguished, aristocratic; because their touch is light, their movement deft and fleet; because they proceed by omission, by implication and suggestion; because they employ the *demi-mot* and the *nuance*; because, in fine, they are Subtle – other books are the Cats of Bookland.

And the Average Man hates them or ignores them.

I have the honour, dear Mr. Editor, to subscribe myself, as ever,

Your obedient servant,

THE YELLOW DWARF.

LETTER 13
CAT VERSUS BIRD

Adlai Stevenson II to the Members of the Senate of the 66th General Assembly

23 April 1949

In 1949, having succumbed to pressure from Friends of Birds, Inc., an organisation formed for the 'promotion of kindness to birds', the Illinois Legislature passed Senate Bill No. 93, titled 'An Act to Provide Protection to Insectivorous Birds by Restraining Cats', which sought to punish financially, up to $5 per violation, those cat owners who allowed their pets to roam free, without a leash. The bill was met largely with ridicule, not least from pet owners who were acutely aware that cats, unlike dogs, would simply not stand for such a thing. Luckily for the cats and their owners, the newly elected Illinois Democratic governor, Adlai Stevenson II, was similarly unimpressed and vetoed the bill with a letter that soon made the news.

THE LETTER

STATE OF ILLINOIS
EXECUTIVE DEPARTMENT
SPRINGFIELD

April 23, 1949

To the Honorable, the Members of the Senate of the Sixty-sixth General Assembly:

I herewith return, without my approval, Senate Bill No. 93, entitled, "An Act to Provide Protection to Insectivorous Birds by Restraining Cats." This is the so-called "Cat Bill." I veto and withhold my approval from this Bill for the following reasons:

It would impose fines on owners or keepers who permitted their cats to run at large off their premises. It would permit any person to capture or call upon the police to pick up and imprison, cats at large. It would permit the use of traps. The bill would have statewide application – on farms, in villages, and in metropolitan centers.

This legislation has been introduced in the past several sessions of the Legislature, and it has, over the years, been the source of much comment – not all of which has been in a serious vein. It may be that the General Assembly has now seen fit to refer it to one who can view it with a fresh outlook. Whatever the reasons for passage at this session, I cannot believe there is a widespread public demand for this law or that it could, as a practical matter, be enforced.

Furthermore, I cannot agree that it should be the declared public policy of Illinois that a cat visiting a neighbor's yard or crossing the highway is a public nuisance. It is in the nature of cats to do a certain amount of unescorted roaming. Many live with their owners in apartments or other restricted premises, and I doubt if we want to make their every brief foray an opportunity for a small game hunt by zealous citizens – with traps or otherwise. I am afraid this Bill could only create discord, recrimination and enmity. Also consider the owner's dilemma: To escort a cat abroad on a leash is against the nature of the cat, and to permit it to venture forth for exercise unattended into a night of new dangers is against the nature of the owner. Moreover, cats perform useful service, particularly in rural areas, in combating rodents – work they necessarily perform alone and without regard for property lines.

We are all interested in protecting certain varieties of birds. That cats destroy some birds, I well know, but I believe this legislation would further but little the worthy cause to which its proponents give such unselfish effort. The problem of cat versus bird is as old as time. If we attempt to resolve it by legislation who knows but what we may be called upon to take sides as well in the age old problems of dog versus cat, bird versus bird, or even bird versus worm. In my opinion, the State of Illinois and its local governing bodies already have enough to do without trying to control feline delinquency.

For these reasons, and not because I love birds the less or cats the more, I veto and withhold my approval from Senate Bill No. 93.

Respectfully,

ADLAI E. STEVENSON

Governor

LETTER 14
THE CAT ORGAN

'Mary Midnight' to the Royal Society

1751

In 1751, a bizarre letter was reprinted in The Midwife *magazine that raised more than a few of its many readers' eyebrows. Addressed to the Royal Society in London (the world's oldest scientific academy) and written by a 'Mary Midnight', it described in great detail the Cat-Organ, a rare musical instrument powered by living, breathing, meowing cats. In actual fact, the letter was satirical, and Mary Midnight was a pseudonym used to comic effect by Christopher Smart, an English poet born in Kent in 1722 who was friends with Samuel Johnson, and who, when he wasn't sending spoof correspondence, put on shows in which he dressed in drag and performed as Mrs Midnight. Life for Smart took a darker turn in 1757, when he was committed to a mental asylum for six years. It was there that he wrote his greatest poetry.*

THE LETTER

GENTLEMEN,

I need not inform persons of your infinite experience and erudition, that the Cat-Organ, as it has hitherto been made use of, was no more than what followeth, viz. A plain harpsichord; which, instead of having strings and jacks, consists of Cats of different sizes, included in boxes, whose voices express every note in the gamut, which is extorted from the imprisoned animals by placing their tails in grooves, which are properly squeezed by the impression of the organist's fingers on the keys. This instrument, unimproved as it was, I have often heard with incredible delight, but especially in the grand and plaintive. This delight grew upon me every time I was present at its performance. At length I shut myself up for seven years, to study some additions and improvements, which I have at length accomplished, agreeable to my warmest wishes; and which I with all due submission now lay before you.

In the first place, then, it is universally known and acknowledged, that these animals, at the time of their amours, are the most musical creatures in nature; I would therefore recommend it to all and singular Cat-Organists, to have a most especial regard to the time of caterwauling, particularly if they have anything very august or affecting to exhibit.

Secondly, it is also very well known that the best voices are improved by castration; I therefore never have less than eight geldings in my treble clef. And here I cannot help informing you of an experiment I lately made on an Italian boar-cat, and an English one of the same gender; and I solemnly protest that, after the operation, my country animal had every whit as delicate, piercing, and comprehensive a tone, as the foreigner: and I make no sort of doubt that some of our harmonious Englishmen would shine with an equal lustre, if they had the same advantages as the Italians. This may be worth the consideration of people in power: for, if this experiment had been tried with success, how many thousand pounds would it have saved this nation!

Thirdly. Of the Forte and Piano. I must not omit to tell you, gentlemen, that my Cat-Organ resembles a double harpsichord; for, as that has two rows of keys, so mine has two layers of Cats, both of a lesser size, and whose tails are squeezed by a much less pressure; that is, by nothing but the bare extremity of the key. But the lower row, on which I play forte, or loudly, contains an harmonious society of banging grimalkins; and whose tails are severely pricked by brass pins, inserted at the end of the key for that purpose.

Fourthly, Of the Shake. There was one enormous defect in this instrument, before I took it in hand, and that was in the shake; the imperfection of which gave me great offence. But, as it is now managed, it has the most ravishing effect in the world. There are between all the keys little wires fixed almost imperceptibly; these go underneath till they reach each puss's throat: at the extremity of these wires are placed horizontally wrens' quills, about the length of a quarter of an inch. When the artist, therefore, has a mind to form his shake, he touches the wires, which soon send the quills in a tickle, tickle, tickle, tickle, up to the Cat's throat, and causes the most gurgling, warbling, shaking, quaking, trembling, murmuring sound, in the world.

Fifthly. Of the Staccato, and an infallible method of keeping the four-footed performers under proper regulations.

This most intolerable deficiency of the old Cat-Organ was as follows: some of the Cats were apt to continue their mew after the proper note was expressed, to the great confusion of the tune, and vexation of the organist. This I have entirely cured; and, I think, I can play the most perfect staccato in the world. I have underneath my instrument a treddle, like that of a spinning-wheel, which I work with my foot: this treddle actuates a certain number of forceps or pincers, which open and shut, at my pleasure, upon the noses and chins of all the Cats; and if any of them over-act their part, I tip St. Dunstan upon Mrs. Puss, and she is obliged of necessity to be silent.

Sixthly. Of the education of Cats for the Organ. My predecessors were egregiously out in this article, as well as many others; which, whatever it may appear to the incredulous or incurious, is a matter of importance. With regard to their diet, milk and flummery, fried mice and fish, have the best effect; I mean, for the trebles and tenors: as for the bases, I have fed them with good success on bullock's liver, hog's harslet's, and sometimes with viands of a much less delicate nature. As for exercise, moderate mousing, and being well tugged and hauled about by the children, will very well suffice.

Mr. Collier, in his Essay on Musick, says – that he makes no doubt that there might be a warlike instrument contrived, of such an hideous sound, that instead of inspiring men with courage, it would strike the most undaunted with dismay. This may be effected by the above-mentioned instrument: for though the Cat-Organ, when accurately in tune, is incomparably melodious, yet it may be so managed, as to utter shrieks very little inferior to the cries of the infernals themselves. Happy that instrument, where terror and transport, ornament and utility, are so exquisitely blended! which, by its persuasive harmony, can at one time draw St. Cecilia from the spheres; and, at another, with proper alteration, would frighten away the devil himself in propriâ personâ!

I am, Gentlemen,

Your most obedient humble Servant.

M. MIDNIGHT

LETTER 15
A PILE OF 5,000 CATS AND KITTENS

Frederick Law Olmsted to his son

13 May 1875

Born in 1822 in Connecticut, Frederick Law Olmsted is considered by many in his profession to be the 'Father of American Landscape Architecture' – a title that seems, even to the least qualified of observers, to be fully justified, for Olmsted had at least a hand in designing some of the most famous urban parks in the US, including, most notably, New York's Central Park. Other commissions consisted of major parkways, reservations, college campuses and government buildings too numerous to list. To his four-year-old son in May of 1875, however, these achievements meant nothing: Henry was miles away from home with his mother and just wanted to see the family dog, Quiz, so he wrote to his father and asked for Quiz to be sent to him. This was his father's inventive reply.

THE LETTER

13th May, 1875

Dear Henry:
The cats keep coming into the yard, six of them every day, and Quiz drives them out. If I should send Quiz to you to drive the cows away from your rhubarb he would not be here to drive the cats out of the yard. If six cats should keep coming into the yard every day and not go out, in a week there would be 42 of them and in a month 180 and before you came back next November 1260. Then if there should be 1260 cats in the yard before next November half of them at least would have kittens and if half of them should have 6 kittens apiece, there would be more than 5000 cats and kittens in the yard. There would not be any place for Rosanna to spread the clothes unless she drove them all off the grass plot, and if she did they would have to crowd at the end of the yard nearest the house, and if they did that they would make a great pile as high as the top of my windows. A pile of 5000 cats and kittens, some of them black ones, in front of my window would make my office so dark I should not be able to write in it. Besides that those underneath, particularly the kittens, would be hurt by

those standing on top of them and I expect they would make such a great squalling all the time that I should not be able to sleep, and if I was not able to sleep, I should not be able to work, and if I did not work I should not have any money, and if I had not any money, I could not send any to Plymouth to pay your fare back on the Fall River boat, and I could not pay my fare to go to Plymouth and so you and I would not ever see each other any more. No, Sir. I can't spare Quiz and you will have to watch for the cows and drive them off yourself or you will raise no rhubarb.

Your affectionate father.

LETTER 16
THE ZOMBI

Robert Southey to Grosvenor Bedford

3 April 1821

For thirty years, beginning in 1813, Robert Southey, friend to Samuel Taylor Coleridge and William Wordsworth, was Poet Laureate of England until his death in 1843. He was also a celebrated biographer of Horatio Nelson, Oliver Cromwell and others, and a tireless writer of criticism, political essays, translations, journalism and letters. He even, in 1837, wrote what is considered to be the first published iteration of the *Goldilocks and the Three Bears* ***fairy tale, titled*** *The Story of the Three Bears* ***and included in an initially anonymously authored volume of his work. Long before that, in November of 1820, Othello, a cat taken in by the Southeys, died, leaving the household both bereft and infinitely more attractive to a local gang of rats. A few months later, Southey wrote to his friend Grosvenor Bedford, with news of Othello's replacement, Zombi.***

THE LETTER

April 3, 1821

MY DEAR G.,

You were duly apprised towards the end of the year of Othello's death. Since that lamented event this house was cat-less, till on Saturday, March 24. Mrs. Calvert, knowing how grievously we were annoyed by rats, offered me what she described as a fine full-grown black cat, who was moreover a tom. She gave him an excellent character in all points but one, which was that he was a most expert pigeon-catcher; and as they had a pigeon house, this propensity rendered it necessary to pass sentence upon him either of transportation or of death. Moved by compassion (his colour and his tomship also being taken into consideration), I consented to give him an asylum, and on the evening of that day here he came in a sack.

You, Grosvenor, who are a *philogalist*, and therefore understand more of cat nature than has been ever attained by the most profound naturalists, know how difficult it is to reconcile a cat to a new domicile. When the sack was opened, the kitchen door, which leads into the passage, was open also, and the cat disappeared; not indeed like a flash of lightning, but as fast as one,— that is to say, for all purposes of a simile. There was no chance of his making his way back to the pigeon house. He might have done this had he been carried thrice the distance in any other direction; but in this there was either a river to cross, or a part of the town to pass, both of which were such obstacles to his travels that we were quite sure all on this side of them was to him *terra incognita*. Food, therefore, was placed where he would be likely to find it in the night; and at the unanimous desire of the children, I took upon myself the charge of providing him with a name, for it is not proper that a cat should remain without one. Taking into consideration his complexion, as well as his sex, my first thought was to call him Henrique Diaz, a name which poor Koster would have approved, had he been living to have heard it; but it presently occurred to me that the Zombi would be an appellation equally appropriate and more dignified. The Zombi, therefore, he was named.

It was soon ascertained that the Zombi had taken possession of poor Wilsey's cellar, which being filled with pea-sticks afforded him a secure hiding-place; the kitchen also of that part of the house being forsaken, he was in perfect quiet. Food was laid for him every day, and the children waited impatiently for the time when the Zombi would become acquainted with the house, and suffer them to become acquainted with him. Once or twice in the evening he was seen out of doors, and it was known that he reconnoitred the premises in the night; but in obstinate retirement he continued from Saturday till Saturday, seven days and nights, notwithstanding all kind words were used to bring him out, as if he had been determined to live and die a hermit.

But between four and five o'clock on the Sunday morning, all who had ears to hear were awakened by such screams as if the Zombi had been caught in a rat-trap, or had met with some other excruciating accident. You, Mr. Bedford, understand cats, and know very well that a cat-*solo* is a very different thing from a *duet*; and that no person versed in their tongue can mistake their expression of pain for anything else. The creature seemed to be in agonies. A light was procured, that it might be relieved if that were possible. Upon searching the house, the Zombi was seen at the top of Wilsey's stairs, from whence he disappeared, retreating to his stronghold in the cellar; nor could any traces be discovered of any hurt that could have befallen him, nor has it since appeared that he had received any, so that the cause of this nocturnal disturbance remains an impenetrable mystery.

Various have been our attempts to explain it. Some of the women who measure the power of rats by their own fears, would have it that he was bitten by a rat, or by an association of rats; but to this I indignantly replied that in that case the ground would have been strewn with their bodies, and that it would have been the rats' cry, not the Zombi's, that would have been heard. Dismissing, therefore, that impossible supposition, I submit to your consideration, in the form of queries, the various possibilities which have occurred to me,— all unsatisfactory, I confess,— requesting you to assist me in my endeavour to find out the mystery of this wonderful history, as it may truly be called. You will be pleased to bear in mind that the Zombi was the only cat concerned in the transaction: of that I am perfectly certain.

Now then, Grosvenor,—

1. Had he seen the devil?
2. Was he making love to himself?
3. Was he engaged in single combat with himself?
4. Was he attempting to raise the devil by invocation?
5. Had he heard me sing, and was he attempting (vainly) to imitate it?

These queries, you will perceive, all proceed upon

the supposition that it was the Zombi who made the noise.

But I have further to ask,—

6. Was it the devil?
7. Was it Jeffery?
8. Were either of these personages tormenting the Zombi?

I have only to add that from that time to this he continues in the same obstinate retirement, and to assure you that

I remain,
Mr. Bedford,
With the highest consideration,
Yours as ever,

ROBERT SOUTHEY

PS. One further query occurs while I am writing, Sunday having been the first of the month—

9. Was he making April fools of us?

R. S.

LETTER 17
BRACE UP HONEY

Gabrielle-Ange Lévesque (his mother) to Jack Kerouac

20 July 1960

In the summer of 1960, a few years after publication of his opus *On the Road,* ***Beat novelist and poet Jack Kerouac left his mother at home in Northport, New York, and headed west to spend a peaceful few months at a cabin in Big Sur that was owned by his friend and fellow poet, Lawrence Ferlinghetti. It was to be a time of relaxation and reflection. When he eventually arrived, however, Kerouac was handed a letter from his mother, sent hurriedly to Ferlinghetti to pass on, containing news of the death of his treasured cat, Tyke. Kerouac later compared this event to the death of his nine-year-old brother in 1926, when Jack was just four years of age.***

THE LETTER

Sunday 20 July 1960

Dear Son,
I'm afraid you wont like my letter because I only have sad news for you right now. I really dont know how to tell you this but Brace up Honey. I'm going through hell myself. Little Tyke is *gone*. Saturday all day he was fine and seemed to pick up strength, but late at night I was watching TV a late movie. Just about 1:30 A.M. when he started belching and throwing up. I went to him and tried to fix him up but to no *availe*. He was shivering like he was cold so I rapped him up in a Blanket then he started to throw up all over me. And that was the last of him. Needless to say how I feel and what I went through. I stayed up till "day *Break*" and did all I could to revive him but it was useless. I realized at 4 A.M. he was gone so at six I wrapped him up good in a clean blanket – and at 7 A.M. went out to dig his grave. I never did anything in my whole life so heart breaking as to bury my beloved little Tyke who was as human as you and I. I buried him under the Honeysuckle vines, the corner, of the fence. I just cant sleep or eat. I keep looking and hoping to see him come

through the cellar door calling *Ma Wow*. I'm just plain sick and the weirdest thing happened when I buried Tyke, all the black Birds I fed all Winter seemed to have known what was going on. Honest Son this is no lies. There was lots and lots of *em* flying over my head and chirping, and settling on the fence, for a whole hour after Tyke was laid to rest – that's something I'll never forget – I wish I had a camera at the time but God and Me knows it and saw it. Now Honey I know this is going to hurt you but I had to tell you somehow . . . I'm so sick not physically but heart sick . . . I just cant believe or realize that my Beautiful little Tyke is no more – and that I wont be seeing him come through his little "Shanty" or Walking through the green grass . . .

PS. I've got to dismantle Tyke's shanty, I just cant go out there and see it empty – as is. Well Honey, write soon again and be kind to yourself. Pray the real "God" –

Your old Mom XXXXXX

‘I KEEP LOOKING
AND HOPING TO SEE
HIM COME THROUGH
THE CELLAR DOOR
CALLING MA WOW.’

– *Gabrielle-Ange Lévesque*

LETTER 18

ODE ON THE DEATH OF A FAVOURITE CAT DROWNED IN A TUB OF GOLDFISHES

Thomas Gray to Horace Walpole

1 March 1747

One day in February 1747, at the home of noted historian Horace Walpole, one of his cats, Selima, decided to perch, as she was wont to do, on the rim of a Chinese porcelain tub that was filled with goldfish – the perfect spot from which to stare into the water and plot an attack. Sadly for all involved – fish included – Selima lost her footing this time, and despite her best efforts slipped all the way in, unable to escape due to the steep sides of the fish-filled trap. One can only imagine the chaos. Selima didn't make it out, and when Walpole was informed of her death, he turned to his friend, the poet Thomas Gray, and asked him to write a fitting epitaph. Gray soon responded with something more substantial, the first verse of which Walpole later had engraved on the fishbowl in which his cat had perished.

THE LETTER

Cambridge,
1 March, 1747

As one ought to be particularly careful to avoid blunders in a compliment of condolence, it would be a sensible satisfaction to me (before I testify my sorrow, and the sincere part I take in your misfortune) to know for certain, who it is that I lament. I knew Zara and Selima (Selima, was it? or Fatima?) or rather I knew both of them together; for I cannot justly say which was which. Then as to your handsome Cat, the name you distinguished her by, I am no less at a loss, as well knowing one's handsome cat is always the cat one likes best; or if one be alive and the other dead, it is usually the latter that is the handsomest. Besides, if the point were never so clear, I hope you do not think me so ill-bred or so imprudent as to forfeit all my interest in the survivor: Oh no! I would rather seem to mistake, and to be sure it must be the tabby one that had met with this sad accident. Till this affair is a little better determined, you will excuse me if I do not begin to cry:

"Tempus inane peto, requiem, spatiumque doloris."

Which interval is the more convenient, as it gives time to rejoice with you on your new honours. This is only a beginning; I reckon next week we shall hear you are a free-Mason, or a Gormorgon at least. Heigh ho! I feel (as you to be sure have done long since) that I have very little to say, at least in prose. Somebody will be the better for it; I do not mean you, but your Cat, feue Mademoiselle Selime, whom I am about to immortalize for one week or fortnight, as follows.

Ode on the Death of a Favourite Cat Drowned in a Tub of Goldfishes

'Twas on a lofty vase's side,
Where China's gayest art had dyed
The azure flowers that blow;
Demurest of the tabby kind,
The pensive Selima, reclin'd,
Gazed on the lake below.

Her conscious tail her joy declar'd:
The fair round face, the snowy beard,
The velvet of her paws,
Her coat, that with the tortoise vies,
Her ears of jet, and emerald eyes,
She saw; and purr'd applause.

Still had she gazed; but 'midst the tide
Two angel forms were seen to glide,
The Genii of the stream;
Their scaly armour's Tyrian hue
Through richest purple to the view
Betray'd a golden gleam.

The hapless Nymph with wonder saw:
A whisker first, and then a claw,
With many an ardent wish
She stretch'd, in vain, to reach the prize.
What female heart can gold despise?
What cat's averse to fish?

Presumptuous maid! with looks intent
Again she stretch'd, again she bent,
Nor knew the gulf between.
(Malignant Fate sat by, and smiled)
The slippery verge her feet beguiled;
She tumbled headlong in.

Eight times emerging from the flood
She mew'd to every watery god
Some speedy aid to send.
No Dolphin came, no Nereid stirr'd,
Nor cruel Tom nor Susan heard–
A favourite has no friend!

From hence, ye Beauties! undeceiv'd,
Know one false step is ne'er retriev'd,
And be with caution bold:
Not all that tempts your wandering eyes
And heedless hearts is lawful prize,
Nor all that glisters gold!

There's a poem for you, it is rather too long for an Epitaph.

LETTER 19
FOSS IS DEAD

Edward Lear to Lord Aberdare

29 November 1887

In 1887 British poet and illustrator Edward Lear wrote to his friend, Lord Aberdare, with some tragic news: Lear's tabby cat, Foss, whom he had owned since kittenhood, was dead. This was not a sad development just for Lear, who was a popular figure during his lifetime, but also for the many fans of Lear who had grown to love Foss through his illustrated appearances in Lear's work. Two months later, Lear died of heart disease. At the head of this letter to Aberdare, in its recipient's hand, is written, 'Last letter from my dear old friend, who died Jan 1888.'

THE LETTER

Villa Tennyson
San Remo
29 November 1887

My dear Lord Aberdare,
I have been wanting to know how your hand is now – if quite recovered, or still giving trouble? But I am little able now a days to write albeit I have a great deal of writing to get through.

For, whoever has known me for 30 years has known that for all that time my Cat Foss has been part of my solitary life.

Foss is dead: & I am glad to say did not suffer at all – having become quite paralyzed on all one side of him. So he was placed in a box yesterday, & buried deep below the Figtree at the end of the Orange walk & tomorrow there will be a stone placed giving the date of his death & his age (31 years,) – (of which 30 were passed in my house.)

> Qui sotto è sepolto il mio buon
> Gatto Foss. Era 30 anni in casa
> mia, e morì il 26 Novembre
> 1887, di età 31 anni

[Here lies buried my good cat Foss. He was 30 years in my house, and died on 26 November 1887, at the age of 31 years.]

All those friends who have known my life will understand that I grieve over this loss. As for myself I am much as usual, only suffering from a very bad fall I had on Novr. 5th – having risen, the Lamp having gone out, & the matches misplaced, so that I could not find them.

The effects of this fall have lasted several days – but now – THANK GOD THURSDAY 29TH are beginning to cause less worry. Salvatore has the stone for Foss, & the Inscription, & I suppose in a day or two all will be as before, except the memory of my poor friend Foss.

> Qui sotto sta seppolito il mio buon
> Gatto Foss. Era 30 anni in casa mia,
> e morì il 26 November 1887— in età
> 31 anni.

[Beneath this stone was buried my good cat Foss. He was 30 years in my house, and died on 26 November 1887 – at 31 years of age.]

Let me know before long how your hand is now. I have lost many friends latterly, among these, Harvie Farquhar, brother of Mrs George Clive.

My love to all of you.

Your's affectionately

Edward Lear

LETTER 20
CAT FANCY

Ayn Rand to *Cat Fancy* magazine

20 March 1966

As well as writing such novels as *Atlas Shrugged* ***and*** *The Fountainhead*, ***Russian-American author Ayn Rand was also responsible for developing the anti-altruistic, pro-selfishness philosophy that ran through them which she later called Objectivism, its core belief being that man's 'highest moral purpose is the achievement of his own happiness, and that he must not force other people, nor accept their right to force him, that each man must live as an end in himself and follow his own rational self-interest'. Ayn Rand also subscribed to*** *Cat Fancy* ***magazine, and in 1966 replied to a question from its editor.***

THE LETTER

March 20, 1966

Dear Miss Smith,

You ask whether I own cats or simply enjoy them, or both. The answer is: both. I love cats in general and own two in particular.

You ask: "We are assuming that you have an interest in cats, or was your subscription strictly objective?" My subscription was strictly objective because I have an interest in cats. I can demonstrate objectively that cats are of a great value, and the charter issue of Cat Fancy magazine can serve as part of the evidence. ("Objective" does not mean "disinterested" or indifferent; it means corresponding to the facts of reality and applies both to knowledge and to values.)

I subscribed to Cat Fancy primarily for the sake of the pictures, and found the charter issue very interesting and enjoyable.

Ayn Rand

LETTER 21
A PITY SUCH FINE CATS SHOULD BE DEAF

William Darwin Fox to Charles Darwin

16 August 1860

Should you ever consider owning a blue-eyed cat with white fur, be warned: the cat will probably be deaf. This happens because of the dominance of the white masking gene, known simply as W, which inhibits three things: pigment production in the skin, resulting in white fur; pigment production in the eyes, resulting in blue eyes; and the growth of certain cells in the inner ear, resulting in impaired hearing. Back in 1868, nine years after publication of his seminal work *On the Origin of Species*, ***world-renowned naturalist Charles Darwin published another book,*** *The Variation of Animals and Plants under Domestication*, ***in which he stated this very fact, saying, 'white cats, if they have blue eyes, are almost always deaf'. He then cited this letter, from his second cousin, Reverend William Darwin Fox, as evidence.***

THE LETTER

My dear Darwin

In answer to your enquiry, I believe I might truly state – not one dozen, but dozens of white cats came under my observation. The first I saw was a half bred Persian at Ryde. I had a kitten of hers, from whom I had a great number, never having less than six at a time for years. In every case, if pure white & with blue eyes, they were stone deaf. I used to show this by making all sorts of the loudest noises close to them, which they never in the least perceived.

I have remarked them in various other places – one at the large Inn at Chichester (which I think was a male) – 2 Norwegian Cats whose owner I amazed (as I have done several others), by remarking "that it was a pity such fine cats should be deaf". These were females.

Of course the greater part of those we bred & kept were females, but I also had males, as I kept my breed pure for many years. I am certain the females were deaf, & I have no doubt about the males being so also, as I must have observed them if they had not been.

I forget where I wrote several letters on the subject of these blue eyed cats – it is now 20 to 30 years since – but they elicited exactly similar facts.

I bred several that had only one eye blue; and

we were quite convinced that in those cases, they were deaf only on the blue side. All my elder children remember "Lily" our first cat – as perfectly deaf & blue eyed – & she certainly brought litters of kittens for many years –

So that the sex is undeniable, tho' I once had a Male Tortoiseshell (or at least so reputed) who had a family – to the great delight of my children.

Ever yours W D Fox

After writing the above I asked my wife & cubs if they remembered the white cats. "Lily" was too far back, but "Glaucops" was well remembered for her azure eyes, and kittens innumerable.

Fanny, who is just returned from Bradwell nr Gt Yarmouth – added "that there is a cat there perfectly white, but with the usual green eyes, that is deaf – like the blue eyed ones." She remarked this particularly, as opposed to the blue eyed theory.

But at Caister Rectory close by Mr Steward has a magnificent blue eyed cat which is quite deaf.

I shall probably see both these cats before long, and shall very likely find a Colony about there.

The Caister Cat – being described as very fine, may probably be a male.

Your son William was kind enough to call here on Friday, and most favourably impressed us all.

LETTER 22
AM I REALLY WRITING IT AT ALL?

Raymond Chandler to Charles Morton

19 March 1945

Author Raymond Chandler was born in Chicago in 1888, and to this day remains one of the greats in the world of crime fiction thanks to his creation of Philip Marlowe, the hardboiled detective who stars in many of his stories: *The Big Sleep* ***(1939)***, *Farewell, My Lovely* ***(1940)***, *The High Window* ***(1942)***, *The Lady in the Lake* ***(1943)***, *The Little Sister* ***(1949)***, *The Long Goodbye* ***(1953) and*** *Playback* ***(1958). Had you approached Chandler's desk at any point during the writing process of these books, chances are you would have spotted Taki, his Persian cat, keeping him company. In March of 1945 Chandler wrote to the associate editor of*** *The Atlantic Monthly*, ***Charles Morton, to introduce him.***

THE LETTER

Paramount Pictures Inc.
5451 Marathon Street
Hollywood 38, Calif.
March 19,1945

Dear Charles:

A man named Inkstead took some pictures of me for *Harper's Bazaar* a while ago (I never quite found out why) and one of me holding my secretary in my lap came out very well indeed. When I get the dozen I have ordered I'll send you one. The secretary, I should perhaps add, is a black Persian cat, 14 years old, and I call her that because she has been around me ever since I began to write, usually sitting on the paper I wanted to use or the copy I wanted to revise, sometimes leaning up against the typewriter and sometimes just quietly gazing out of the window from a corner of the desk, as much as to say, "The stuff you're doing's a waste of my time, bud." Her name is Taki (it was originally Take, but we got tired of explaining that this was a Japanese word meaning bamboo and should be pronounced in two syllables), and she has a memory like no elephant ever even tried to have. She is usually politely remote, but once in a while will get an argumentative spell and talk back for ten minutes at a time. I wish I knew what she is trying to say then, but I suspect it all adds up to a very sarcastic version of "You can do better." I've been a cat lover all my life (have nothing against dogs except that they need such a lot of entertaining) and have never quite been able to understand them. Taki is a completely poised animal and always knows who likes cats, never goes near anybody that doesn't, always walks straight up to anyone, however lately arrived and completely unknown to her, who really does. She doesn't spend a great deal of time with them, however, just takes a moderate amount of petting and strolls off. She has another curious trick (which may or may not be rare) of never killing anything. She brings 'em back alive and lets you take them away from her. She has brought into the house at various times such things as a dove, a blue parakeet, and a large butterfly. The butterfly and the parakeet were entirely unharmed and carried on just as though nothing had happened. The dove gave her a little trouble, apparently not wanting to be carried around, and had a small spot of blood on its breast. But we took it to a bird man and it was all right very soon. Just a bit humiliated. Mice bore her, but she catches them if they insist and then I have to kill them. She has a sort of tired interest in gophers, and will watch a gopher hole with some attention, but gophers bite and after all who the hell wants a gopher anyway? So she just pretends she might catch one, if she felt like it.

She goes with us wherever we go journeying, remembers all the places she has been to before and is usually quite at home anywhere. One or two places have got her – I don't know why. She just wouldn't settle down in them. After a while we know enough to take the hint. Chances are there was an axe murder there once and we're much better somewhere else. The guy might come back. Sometimes she looks at me with a rather peculiar expression (she is the only cat I know who will look you straight in the eye) and I have a suspicion that she is keeping a diary, because the expression seems to be saying: "Brother, you think you're pretty good most of the time, don't you? I wonder how you'd feel if I decided to publish some of the stuff I've been putting down at odd moments." At certain times she has a trick of holding one paw up loosely and looking at it in a speculative manner. My wife thinks she is suggesting we get her a wrist watch; she doesn't need it for any practical reason – she can tell the time better than I can – but after all you gotta have some jewelry.

I don't know why I'm writing all this. It must

be I couldn't think of anything else, or – this is where it gets creepy – am I really writing it at all? Could it be that – no, it must be me. Say it's me. I'm scared.

Ray

LETTER 23
CATS, CATS, CATS OF MINE

Ester Krumbachová to her cats

5 July 1985

Aran, Bajaja, Beanie, Crayon, Johánek, Mauglí, Misha, Petinka, Piggy, Snail, Starlet, Uki . . . Ester Krumbachová was never without a cat, and she believed there was no deeper connection than the bond that existed between she and her feline companions. Born in 1923, Krumbachová was an important figure in Czech New Wave cinema, a visionary who made her mark quietly, behind the scenes, as a costume designer and screenwriter on many celebrated films of the era. She died in 1996, aged seventy-two, without the level of recognition she deserved. In her archives can be found this letter, written in 1985 when she was sixty-one and, she felt, approaching her final lap, addressed to the many cats with whom she had shared her life.

THE LETTER

PRAGUE, 5 JULY, 1985

Cats, cats, cats of mine,
I saw you being born and I saw you dying. I saw your lives in their entirety; companions of my life. I saw your little paws learning how to walk and I saw them slowly petrifying as you were dying. I saw your beautiful and wild eyes sparkling when they opened for the first time and I saw them fading out and closed forever. I saw you healthy and joyful and young and I saw you getting old and ill, feeble and pitiful. Your eyes were shining until the last moment, sight fixed to a place somewhere beyond the life we spent together. I stroked your fur when you were little kittens and I stroked your fur before I duly buried you in the ground.

I saw your gentle sense of humour and fun-loving characters and how much reserved hope you put into me. When I was too busy I chased you away when you were hungry for a touch of my hand which was always as tender as you were. You, cats of mine, have taught me many, many incommunicable things. I saw how you craved for a wild hunt, a prey to be caught, a murder as nature determined it. You did not get this chance when you lived together with me; you had no chance to live the lives for which you were born, the lives with true meaning. You were deprived of the animal beauty, of the cruelty, which was nothing other than a word, because you were born as beasts of prey ready to hunt and it was I who deprived you of this. I wish I could have offered you this opportunity! But I was not able to do so.

I left you and you suffered because you were faithful and honest like all animals; like all that beauty in the jungle of life. You gave me hope in horrible sleepless nights. Whenever you sensed with your miraculous internal devices that I was feeling deadly miserable you walked to me silently on your silken feet to ask how long this would last. You put your heads in my palms when I was sleeping and I could feel your tenderness as well as your loneliness. You lay on top of me waking me with a faint noise as if you were calling to me: get up and walk! You worried about me, my dear friends, my sweethearts. You pushed me to be more responsible and care better for my own life.

And this was our joint action, our common affair. My dear cats! You have accompanied me through all my life. Your eyes were so sparkling and questioning, they were filled with tenderness, sometimes you turned them away when I felt too unwell to be able to co-exist with you and reciprocate in the same way you looked at me – you always understood and sustained, you cats of mine. I love you with all my heart and soul. I love you more than anybody else I have ever loved. I have always been faithful to you because I have never been, and never will be able to betray you. I imprisoned you in my flat – a prison of love. I hope you never understood that it was a prison. You were dying and until the last moment you knew you were the loved ones – or perhaps you knew that in the cat's prison for life I was the nicest prison guard, didn't you???

One day I'll find out. I wish for someone to pet me when I die like I petted your bodies. Or better not. I do not wish this, I don't need it. Nevertheless I do believe, my dear pets, that I have done all I could for the love we shared, everything my heart told me to do because it has been and always will be yearning for such a big devotion, like that between you and me. Cats! Cats! You were the most faithful, shy, bashful, reserved, loving, offended, defiant, funny, sad, healthy, old, tired of life and diseases – each of you made up its own world, each of you was a remarkable character, each of you had its own way to approach me, to get closer to me, to play, to make fun and raise hope that together we would make it and survive.

You pressed against me so hard that it woke me up from my exhausting sleep in those days when I felt really down, however, I knew you felt even worse because you were passing away and only came to experience once more the moment of trust, hope and love. My dear deceased friends, who would count your number? You are not dead, when you have gone, it's me who has gone with you. When I saw you in my dream, little Snail, you were running to me, turning away so shyly and timidly as if you were not sure whether you wanted to be petted or not; I cried when I woke up and called at you to give my regards to Beanie who died of grief when you had died because she was unable to live without you and died one morning spread out at her favourite place. I'm sure you'll pass my message to her. Wait for me there when I'll have to go too.

My dear cats! You will wait for me there, won't you? We will play: little Snail will sit on a mighty branch of the tree of paradise and will gently swing the way he always liked to, pretending he doesn't see me. His whole naive face will radiate strange inner sadness and at the same time there will be a light, shy smile. Beanie will play with her own tail, getting ready for a party. Petinka will look at me with his eyes the colour of frosty grapes in early autumn, shifting his weight from one leg to another while his sparkling eyes, filled with tenderness, will welcome me. Johánek will stare at me. Starlet, who died after a cruel veterinary intervention and did not bite my hand even though she felt the need to bite something because of the pain, will look at me like a lost kitten. She knows that I held her in my lap when the pain got unbearable and stayed awake with her till morning when she passed away. Uki will laugh and run back and forth, his tail coiled into a funny question mark, and he will be shy like little Snail's true son, and he will pretend that he wants to run away but eventually he will let me stroke his tummy as he used to in the part of the hall I called Strokers' Corner – like the Speakers' Corner. Mauglí, pompously walking around, will shout at all the others that she was first, as she did her whole life. Poor Misha will be shy and timid. I lost him because he was killed. Someone must have been shooting, particularly targeting cats, to keep up the world's morale. There is no place for cats because they hunt. And the shooter ate roasted goose, duck, chicken, and perhaps as he was shooting he stuffed his mouth with veal, which was also born on this earth. And then many other cats will join in, my friends whom I gave a bit of hope to or found new homes for. My cats, cats, cats! The guides of my life! Because of you I never dared to leave for a long time, as it might be unjust to you – nonetheless it did happen because I was short of money. When you welcomed me after my return you were worried and nervous, even though you had been looked after by a girl who stayed over; you worried whether it was really me. And it was me who called from New Zealand where, among all the strangers, I worried about you every day I stayed there, and therefore I wanted to know whether you were still alive, whether nothing had happened to you, but you, my dear cats, couldn't have known all this. But you knew very well when I was to come back and they said you had been sitting at the door three days before my arrival, patiently waiting. On the plane I recited a great prayer: cats of mine, I'll see you again in three days' time. You will wait for me, won't you? Grass will grow everywhere around and together we will have a lot of fun.

What do you think, Johánek, whom I found on the street? What do you think Starlet, Uki, Misha and my dearest Petinka – I used to call you Van Gogh because you were so special, unique, ginger and white that I even wrote a book about you, hopefully someone will publish it one day. And what about you Mauglí, you will walk in pompously, wagging your broken tail like a doggie, your eyes will sparkle like ocean lagoons again, won't they?? Death is but a thin veil. I'll come too and I will be attractive and will run happily towards you, my cats. We will do the best bits together; I'll be pulling the string or the Bad Toy which always gently hits your noses or ears because it's a rubber band. Oh, I have forgotten Piggy, who disappeared when I left home a long time ago. When I returned home to stay for a short time, Piggy greeted me and laid down in his basket next to the bed watching me with a painful, reproachful and questioning look. After my next departure he left forever. Piggy, you will be there too, won't you? You were a brave lad who jumped out from the first floor straight onto the street to play with the sweeper's broom. Piggy the prankster, the joker. You were a poor and dirty street cat, but you always behaved like an aristocratic tomcat. I picked all your fleas with my fingers – and then I had to leave, my poor little boy. I still have a bad conscience because of what I did to you, Piggy, but I had to earn money; I was a student in those days.

As you know, my cats, my inspiration, my great love and Muses, I had to leave you and your eyes from time to time. When we are together again somewhere where it will be easy to explain everything, you'll forgive me, won't you. Do you remember, Petinka, when you wanted a cuddle that I often used to say: Esti, your friend, must work now,

Petinka, so we have something to EAT. By this I mostly meant you, Petinka; children were throwing you half-dead onto a coal heap in the yard next to the house and you, a ginger and white, skinny kitten, were close to death and needed to be fed a lot. When you sat next to me on a chair by the fridge with your little front paw lifted, watching me with your questioning grey-green eyes, I couldn't resist their beauty and took an immediate decision that you would never ever again encounter fear and misery. Then in your whole life you never wanted to go out, to the outside world, am I correct or not? When we were lying next to each other close to the electric heater, and I longed so much to be a child again, I told you fairy tales and you laughed until you recovered, even though the vet didn't give us much hope. I loved you so much; you were scrawny and lame and I laid you down in a little armchair and covered you with a blanket so that you felt cosy as if you were in a bed and I fed you with egg yolks and wine sugar on the tip of my finger. Later you became a strong and big tomcat and whenever I was working you couldn't wait until I finished and we would be TOGETHER again. In bed we looked at each other earnestly. First I called you Petrushka and later Péti. Be there too, please, when I come to join you. And don't be jealous of little Snail, as you know, he was a lad from the forest, the son of a semi-wild cat; you used to bully him and Snail was such a shy boy. Mauglí loved you and after you were gone, she spent whole nights at the place you used to lay down. Her grief broke my heart. She was missing you so much even though Snail fathered her kittens; well, sit down next to Mauglí as you used to in the kitchen and wait until I come. Will you?

Mauglí was survived by two offspring, the brothers Crayon and Bajaja. They love each other in the same way that you, little Snail, were beloved by Beanie, you child. And there's also Aran, an intelligent and beautiful calico cat, whom I found at the nearby cemetery, tiny and half-frozen. All of them will be gone before me, at least I hope so. I'll be able to cope with the grief. They are old. Me too.

Cats of mine, please make a guard of honour for me when I pass away. I beg you. I don't have better company; there's nobody else I would write a letter like this to, my pets, my friends, who saved me from despair in the worst times. Come meet me!

My best regards to all of you. We all discovered the incommunicable within ourselves, we found each other and we loved each other.

Yours

Ester

LETTER 24
A HOME THAT NEVER CHANGETH

Katherine Mansfield to Ida Baker

20 March 1921

As 1917 came to a close, New Zealand author Katherine Mansfield discovered she had tuberculosis, the disease which would ultimately lead to her death six years later, aged thirty-four. In those years after the diagnosis, she left her home and cats, Athy and Wingley, in England and divided her time between France and Switzerland where she rested, wrote and searched for a cure. In March 1921 she received word from Ida Baker – her close friend, housekeeper and, near the end of Mansfield's life, carer – that Wingley, who had been missing, was now found. This was Mansfield's reply. Days later, she wrote to Elizabeth Bibesco, the lady who was having an affair with Mansfield's husband, and warned her off. Baker soon arrived in France with Wingley in tow – her other cat, Athy, had moved in with an elderly neighbour back in England and, in true feline style, steadfastly refused to leave.

THE LETTER

Villa Isola Bella,
Menton,
France

Sunday.

D.I.

Your telegram about Wingley came late last night. It was very thrilling. I long to know how he was found, and even more, if possible, what was the meeting like between Athy and him. I envy you seeing that. I hope you really saw it and can tell me what happened. It is a great triumph to have found him. But now the question is – what to do with them? If we were not leaving for Switzerland I wouldn't hesitate. But all these train journeys – arriving at hotels, and so on? Would it be torture for cats? I feel the cats' first need is a settled home; a home that never changeth. And I know that is just what I am not going to have. At the same time the idea that they should be destroyed is *horrible!* You see, just suppose you and I hear, when we are in Switzerland, of another place & decide to try it. Or decide to make a sea voyage. Or . . . so much is possible. We couldn't ever leave the cats with Jack, & to take cats where they are not wanted is cruelty. I confess I don't see a way out. If Richard were older Id suggest asking him to mind them. Id better leave it like this. If when you have thought it over you decide it would be an unhappy life for them or impractical for you – have them destroyed.

Elizabeth Bibesco has shown signs of life again. A letter yesterday begging him to resist Katherine. "You have withstood her so gallantly so far how can you give way now". And "you swore nothing on earth should ever come between us". From the letter I feel they are wonderfully suited and I hope he will go on with the affair. He wants to. "How can I exist without your literary advice", she asks. That is a very fascinating question. I shall write to the silly little creature & tell her I have no desire to come between them only she must not make love to him while he is living with me, because that is undignified. He'll never break off these affairs, tho', and I dont see why he should. I wish hed take one on really seriously – and leave me. Every day I long more to be alone.

[. . .]

Take things easy – & look after yourself. I hope the little boy is better.

Yours
Katherine.

LETTER 25
HE EATS LIKE A GENTLEMAN

Florence Nightingale to Mrs Frost

13 December 1875

Florence Nightingale, the founder of modern nursing, dedicated her life to the care of others. In 1854 she took thirty-eight British nurses to Turkey and trained them to tend to the countless victims of the Crimean War. Six years later, she founded a nursing school at London's St Thomas' Hospital – the first of its kind. She also wrote *Notes on Nursing*, ***an influential educational text that is still in print to this day. Despite such a full life, Nightingale found time and energy to care for more than sixty cats over the years, and in December of 1875 she wrote this charming letter to a Mrs Frost about Mr White, a well-behaved cat she had recently given up for adoption.***

THE LETTER

35 South St 13 Dec 1875

Dear Mrs. Frost,

Mrs. Wilson is so good as to invite me to write to you about my Angora Tom-cat (who answers to the name of Mr. *White*) – now hers.

1. Mr. White has never made a dirt in his life: but he has been brought up to go *to a pan*, with sand in it. You must have patience with him, please, till he has been taught to go out-of-doors for his wants.
2. He has always been shut up *at night*: (in a large pantry:) to prevent his being lost. And I believe he ought always to be shut up at night: for this reason. [I think you must keep him in the house for two or three days till he knows his kind mistresses: & the place: for fear he should run away & try to get back to me.]

   And perhaps if you could give him a pan with sand in it for the first night or two, it might be better.
3. He has always been used to have his meals by himself like a gentleman on a plate put upon a 'table-cloth' (on old newspaper) spread on the floor.

   He is not greedy: has never stolen anything: & never drags his bones off his newspaper. But I am sorry to say he has always lived well: he has bones, & milk, in the morning: after 7 o'clock dinner he has any remains of fish not fish bones or chicken – or game-bones: which he eats like a gentleman off a plate in my room, as I have described: & never asks for more – then a little broken meat, & milk, when he is shut up at night:

& a large jar of fresh water (which he can't upset) always on the floor for him.

4. He is the most affectionate & intelligent cat I have ever had: is much fonder of the society of *Christians* than of cats: likes of all things to be above in a room with me: (but make acquaintance with the little dog of a baby friend of ours): & when his own little sister cat died, he refused food & almost broke his heart. He washes & dresses two little kits we have here (of his) himself. I never saw a Tom-cat do this before.
5. You will see Mr. White is very *black* now. But, when he is in the country, he is as white as the driven snow.

He is 10 months old.

I have written a long letter about him: but in short I recommend him to your kind care: & am

yours faithfully

Florence Nightingale

‘HE IS THE MOST
AFFECTIONATE
& INTELLIGENT
CAT I HAVE
EVER HAD.’

– Florence Nightingale

LETTER 26
A TALE OF HORROR

Jane Welsh Carlyle to Kate Stanley

28 December 1860

Jane Baillie Welsh was born in 1801 in Haddington, Scotland, and in 1826 married renowned Scottish philosopher Thomas Carlyle. Their marriage was largely an unhappy one, as evidenced in the thousands of letters they wrote to each other during the forty years they remained wed until her death in 1866, and it is clear that she was often incredibly lonely. Perhaps as a result, she surrounded herself with pets that included cats, dogs and canaries – a mixture sure to lead to problems. Shortly after Christmas in 1860, she wrote to her friend, Kate Stanley, and described a 'tale of horror'.

THE LETTER

5 Cheyne Row Chelsea Friday

Darling!
What a bright, good thought of yours, to write me a Xmas letter! Bless your little Heart and all it cares for!

I think there must have been spiritual magnetism at work; more or less. For I had been wanting to write to *you*, for a good while back; to tell you a 'Tale of Horror' about the Canary! and should have anticipated your letter; but that the end of the year brings me always such a heap of letters to be written *in the Course of Nature*, and little parcels to be made up for old friends [in] the North, which (*not* the friends but the parcels) have come, by length of habit to be a sort of moral necessity. Then these duties (such as they are) have this year had to be "pursued under difficulties" – a severe cold; involving confinement to the house. For the first touch of frost as usual knocked me over – like a nine-pin!

[. . .]

But you are thinking all the while; "what is it about the Canary? – Has *the Cat*–? "–*Eaten* it; you would ask; and the question is by no means an irrelevant one! – No – my Dear! your Canary is not quite eaten; but I am bound to say; no other Canary past, present, or to come, ever had such an affair with a Cat, and came out of it *without being eaten*. Nor could this one, unless *your* Guardian Angel, or mine, or the Canary's own had worked a miracle on its behalf!

The Cat had taken to *studying* the Bird, at its first elevation, with a degree of interest that made one's blood run cold! so I had sent for the Carpenter, and made him suspend the cage from the Drawing-room ceiling with a pully and brass chain. That done, I had no misgivings about leaving the Two alone together; having no idea what a Cat, under the influence of strong desire was *up to*! Returning from my walk one forenoon I was met at the door by Charlotte in the wildest excitement! "Oh! she said, *whatever* do you think the Cat has gone and done?" – "Eaten my Canary"? I answered, with calm desperation, – "No! FAR WORSE"! "She must have sprung off the little table on to the cage, and dragged it down, for the chain is lying in a hundred pieces! and the table is tilted over, and broken in two! and oh! Lady Airlie's basket is broken to shivers! and the *ferns all about*! and the glass cover is broken to shivers! and every thing is all over the carpet"! – "And the Bird safe?" – "Well yes – tho' the cage door was wide open, she hadn't staid to eat it! The noise of the *lead* and everything falling must have frightened herself; for I met *her* rushing down the stairs, as I ran up at the row"!

What a mess when I entered the Drawing room! for "the Row" had just come off, and nothing was cleared away yet; the cage on its side still, on the floor; the table in two separate pieces; the carpet strewn with earth, and ferns, and bird seed, and water, and fragments of earthen ware, glass, brass-chain &c &c! and amidst all the Bird hopping about rather grave, but otherwise "as well as could be expected." I was very sorry about my ferns; for they too were a sort of live pets, and had been given me when I was confined, spring gone a year, by Lady Airlie.

The Cat probably *had* not only frightened herself, but hurt herself, in the general crash of doom she had unexpectedly created. For she had rushed right out at the back door, and never showed herself for 24 hours after, tho a most domestic cat in general.

Relying (Ah too much) on the analogy between feline fools and human ones, I hoped Experience would have taught this individual fool wisdom! So did not at once send the Canary out of the House; seeing that the Cat herself could not be put away –

for both practical and sentimental reasons. on the practical hand, We are never catless for a single week but hosts of very little mice troop in to us, out of the drains. Not only does this Cat keep us free of the mice, but she is cleanly, and moral, and honest – except under the temptation of a live Bird. Then, on the sentimental hand; was she not loved by my little Dog, as tho' she had been his own Sister or wedded Wife? stirring him up to games of romps in his old age, and the chief delight of his old age! For *his* dear little sake, I couldnt put her away!

So a second time I sent for the carpenter; and had the cage fixed up against the window shutter at the very top – the brass chains of the present day, being it seems (as Mr C says) "*like every thing else*, an article that the man who made them ought to have been hanged for"!

The cat pretending to take no further notice of the Bird, I thought she had made up her mind that attempts on its life were not only perilous but hopeless, but one night while I was saying something to Charlotte, She suddenly Sprang at *one perpendicular leap* to the cage and hung on to it with her claws!! I couldnt have believed in such a leap if I hadn't seen it! I flung my sofa cushions at her, and screamed, and frightened her into dropping down. But I kept the poor Bird under lock and key, after that, till I found her a safer home.

Miss Farrers Bird had escaped out of the window one day, and its pretty cage was swinging empty, so I sent the poor thing there, where it is now enjoying a life without shocks! I was very sorry to part with the Bird but should have been far sorrier to have it *eaten*.

[. . .]

My kindest regards and the best of good wishes to Lady Stanley and your sisters and self

Affectionately yours

Jane Carlyle

Remember me to the white Dogs

LETTER 27
HE IS NOT A FORGIVING CAT

John Cheever to Josephine Herbst

6 December 1963

One afternoon in 1960, a balding cat named Blackie was thrust upon novelist John Cheever by Josephine (Josie) Herbst, an old friend who while visiting for lunch explained that she could no longer keep him. Cheever reluctantly homed the cat and renamed him Delmore after the poet Delmore Schwartz, the former wife of whom had once owned the cat in question. Alas, Cheever and Delmore didn't get on; so much so that Cheever's friendship with Herbst soon deteriorated and they ceased contact. The rift finally healed in 1963, when Cheever sent her an update by letter.

THE LETTER

Cedar Lane
Ossining

Some Friday

Dear Josie,

It's been years since we had anything but the most sketchy communication. I've long since owed you an account of the destiny of your cat and here we go.

The cat, after your leaving him, seemed not certain of his character or his place and we changed his name to Delmore which immediately made him more vivid. The first sign of his vividness came when he dumped a load in a Kleenex box while I was suffering from a cold. During a paroxysim of sneezing I grabbed for some kleenex. I shall not overlook my own failures in this tale but when I got the cat shit off my face and the ceiling I took Delmore to the kitchen door and drop-kicked him into the clothesyard. This was an intolerable cruelty and I have not yet been forgiven. He is not a forgiving cat. Indeed he is proud. The next eventfulness came on Thanksgiving. When the family had gathered for dinner and I was about to carve the turkey there came a strangling noise from the bathroom. I ran there and found Delmore sitting in the toilet, neck-deep in cold water and very sore. I got him out and dried him with towels but there was no forgiveness. Shortly after Christmas a Hollywood writer and his wife came to lunch. My usual salutation to Delmore is Up your's, and when the lady heard me say this she scorned me and gathered Delmore to her breasts. Delmore, in a flash, started to unscrew her right eyeball and the lady, trying to separate herself from Delmore lost a big piece of an Italian dress she was wearing which Mary said cost $250.00. This was not held against Delmore and a few days later when we had a skating party I urged Delmore to come to the pond with us. he seemed pleased and frisked along like a family-loving cat but at that moment a little wind came from the northeast and spilled the snow off a hemlock onto Delmore. he gave me a dirty look, went back to the house and dumped another load into the kleenex box. This time he got the cleaning-woman and they remain unfriendly.

This is not meant at all to be a rancorous account and I think Delmore enjoys himself. I have been accused of cruelty and a woman named Ruth Hershberger keeps writing Elizabeth Pollet, telling her to take the cat away from me, but Delmore contributes a dynamic to all our relationships. People who dislike me go directly to his side and he is, thus, a peace-maker. He loves to play with toilet paper. He does not like catnip mice. He does not kill song birds. In the spring the rabbits chase him around the lawn but they leave after the lettuce has been eaten and he has the terrace pretty much to himself. He is very fat these days and his step, Carl Sandberg not withstanding, sounds more like that of a barefoot middle-aged man on his way to the toilet than the settling in of a winter fog but he has his role and we all respect it and here endeth my report on Delmore the cat.

I hope all is well with you. Mary teaches, I write, the children go to various schools and all is well.

Best,
John

PERMISSION CREDITS

Every effort has been made to trace copyright holders and obtain their permission for the use of copyright material. The publisher apologises for any errors or omissions and would be grateful if notified of any corrections that should be incorporated in future reprints or editions of this book.

LETTER 2 *Always, Rachel: The Letters of Rachel Carson and Dorothy Freeman 1952–1964*. Copyright © 1995 by Roger Allen Christie. Reprinted by permission of Frances Collin, Trustee.

LETTER 3 Jack Lemmon™ used with permission by the Lemmon Family Trust.

LETTER 5 reprinted with kind permission of The Estate of Sylvia Townsend Warner. Reply reprinted by kind permission of United Agents on behalf of the Executor of the Estate of David Garnett.

LETTER 6 reprinted by kind permission of Erik Reece.

LETTER 8 excerpt(s) from *The Diary of a Young Girl: The Definitive Edition* by Anne Frank, edited by Otto H. Frank and Mirjam Pressler, translated by Susan Massotty, translation copyright © 1995 by Penguin Random House LLC. Used by permission of Doubleday, an imprint of the Knopf Doubleday Publishing Group, a division of Penguin Random House LLC. All rights reserved / 264 words from *The Diary of a Young Girl: The Definitive Edition* by Anne Frank, edited by Otto H Frank and Mirjam Pressler, translated by Susan Massotty. English translation copyright © Doubleday a division of Bantam Doubleday Dell Publishing Group Inc, 1995 / Copyright © Anne Frank Tagebuch. Einzig autorisierte und ergänzte Fassung Otto H. Frank und Mirjam Pressler. © 1991 by ANNE FRANK-Fonds, Basel. Alle Rechte vorbehalten S. Fischer Verlag GmbH, Frankfurt am Main.

LETTER 10 From *The Letters of T.S. Eliot* by T.S. Eliot, reprinted by permission of Faber and Faber Ltd / copyright © 2011 Yale University Press all rights reserved. From *The Letters of T.S. Eliot* by T.S. Eliot.

LETTER 11 reprinted by permission of House of Taylor.

LETTER 17 letter by Jack Kerouac's mother by Ms. Kerouac. Copyright © 1960, The Estate of Jack Kerouac, used by permission of The Wylie Agency (UK) Limited.

LETTER 20 Ayn Rand letter from Letters of Ayn Rand. Reprinted with kind permission of Ayn Rand Archives of the Ayn Rand Institute.

LETTER 22 from *Selected Letters of Raymond Chandler*. Published by Dell Publishing, 1987. Copyright © Raymond Chandler. Reproduced by permission of the author c/o Rogers, Coleridge & White Ltd., 20 Powis Mews, London W11 1JN.

LETTER 23 letter to cats of Ester Krumbachová was published in *The First Book of Ester* (Primus, Prague, 1994). From the online Ester Krumbachová Archive (esterkrumbachova.org). Translation: Marta Nedvědická, Guy Tabachnick Courtesy: Ivo Paik and Are | are-events.org

LETTER 24 copyright © The Estate of Katherine Mansfield 1996 from *The Collected Letters of Katherine Mansfield Volume IV: 1920–1921* by Katherine Mansfield. Reproduced with permission of the Oxford Publishing Limited through PLSclear.

LETTER 27 From *The Letters of John Cheever* edited by Benjamin Cheever. Copyright © 1988 by Benjamin Cheever. Reprinted with the permission of Touchstone, a division of Simon & Schuster, Inc. All rights reserved / From *The Letters of John Cheever* by John Cheever. Published by Jonathan Cape. Reprinted by permission of The Random House Group Limited. © 1989 / Copyright © Benjamin Cheever, 1988, used by permission of The Wylie Agency (UK) Limited.

ACKNOWLEDGEMENTS

It requires a dedicated team of incredibly patient people to bring the *Letters of Note* books to life, and this page serves as a heartfelt thank you to every single one of them, beginning with my wife, Karina – not just for kickstarting my obsession with letters all those years ago, but for working with me as Permissions Editor, a vital and complex role. Special mention, also, to my excellent editor at Canongate Books, Hannah Knowles, who has somehow managed to stay focused despite the problems I have continued to throw her way.

Equally sincere thanks to all of the following: the one and only Jamie Byng, whose vision and enthusiasm for this series has proven invaluable; all at Canongate Books, including but not limited to Rafi Romaya, Kate Gibb, Vicki Rutherford and Leila Cruickshank; my dear family at Letters Live: Jamie, Adam Ackland, Benedict Cumberbatch, Aimie Sullivan, Amelia Richards and Nick Allott; my agent, Caroline Michel, and everyone else at Peters, Fraser & Dunlop; the many illustrators who have worked on the beautiful covers in this series; the talented performers who have lent their stunning voices not just to Letters Live, but also to the *Letters of Note* audiobooks; Patti Pirooz; every single archivist and librarian in the world; everyone at Unbound; the team at the Wylie Agency for their assistance and understanding; my foreign publishers for their continued support; and, crucially, my family, for putting up with me during this process.

Finally, and most importantly, thank you to all of the letter writers whose words feature in these books.

ALSO AVAILABLE

LETTERS OF NOTE: FATHERS

LETTERS OF NOTE: MOTHERS

LETTERS OF NOTE: ART

LETTERS OF NOTE: LOVE

LETTERS OF NOTE: WAR

LETTERS OF NOTE: MUSIC

LETTERS OF NOTE: CATS

PENGUIN BOOKS

Ready to find your next great read? Let us help. Visit prh.com/nextread